Jonas Abraham Davis

Judaism Excelled

The tale of a conversion from Judaism to Christianity

Jonas Abraham Davis

Judaism Excelled
The tale of a conversion from Judaism to Christianity

ISBN/EAN: 9783337088910

Printed in Europe, USA, Canada, Australia, Japan

Cover: Foto ©Lupo / pixelio.de

More available books at **www.hansebooks.com**

JUDAISM EXCELLED:

OR THE

𝕮𝖆𝖑𝖊 𝖔𝖋 𝖆 𝕮𝖔𝖓𝖛𝖊𝖗𝖘𝖎𝖔𝖓

FROM

JUDAISM TO CHRISTIANITY:

BEING THE

AUTO-BIOGRAPHY

OF

JONAS ABRAHAM DAVIS.

~~~~~~~~~~~

"God having provided some better thing for us.
The law has become our school-master to bring us unto Christ.
I obtained mercy because I did it ignorantly in unbelief."
—*The Leading Convert from Hebrew Traditionalism*

~~~~~~~~~~~

SECOND EDITION—Revised and Rewritten.

PHILADELPHIA:
PRINTED FOR THE AUTHOR BY J A. WAGENSELLER
No. 23 North Sixth Street, above Market.
1869.

To ALL ISRAELITES indeed,

Those who welcome the "consolation of Israel;"

To all TRUE CHRISTIANS,

Distributed among divers denominations,

Yet alike animated by the apostolic spirit

Which breathes its "hearty desire and prayer to God

That Israel may be saved;"

To the INNUMERABLE COMPANY of eager ears

That have listened with manifest interest,

Shown in abundant smiles and tears,

Whenever from time to time I have felt free

To "declare what God hath done for my soul:"

And with these,

To the large number of PERSONAL FRIENDS,

Whose kindly whispers have conspired

To urge the writing of a history

That pleased them in the relating;

To my FELLOW-LABORER in Christ,

The Rev. J. H. APPLETON,

Whose warm interest in behalf of my dear nationality

Vies with his esteem and assistance in favor of myself;

And to ALL WHO PRAY

That MESSIAH may be CROWNED "LORD OF ALL,"

I AFFECTIONATELY DEDICATE

This Second Edition of my Auto-Biography.

CONTENTS.

———

ITEM OF CORRESPONDENCE.

———

Rev. J. A. Davis:

  Dear Brother,—

    How well do we remember when you, as a stranger *apparently* uncouth, first came to our house. It was in that eventful Spring of 1868. Your excellent credentials—then our only security —laid a recognized claim on the fruits of the season found with us. But how did you, albeit unconsciously, ingratiate yourself in our affections, while yet declining the hospitalities that so fitly offered themselves for your continued use! And as if in consistency, how have you since hastened to maturity, yet so slightly gratified, a friendship that feeds upon our hearts as though it would devour them quite to fatten our friend.

  Your book in its flowing manuscript dress, though it came seeking scrutiny, proved an acceptable proxy. It is so like yourself—permit the acknowledgment— so simple and straightforward. Enlivened throughout by its author's peculiar humor, it is sometimes most refreshing in style, yet never exhibits the slightest straining for effect. That artlessness, with which we should expect a sire to roll out the story of his life, is the reigning spirit here. We can thoroughly trust the record, while pleased with its meandering.

Certainly a somewhat tragic impressiveness is imparted to the pages by the insight they give to the radical revolution which thoroughly transforms the total being of a Jew to the full stature of a Christian. How strange that such throes attend a transition designed from the beginning and demanded as the necessary and only complement of the infantile dispensation—a transition possible too in the easiest and smoothest manner, if the Judaism in question be but genuine and rightly understood. Why then a catastrophe, as preliminary to the change? Every leaf of the narrative gives instant, vivid answer. Accordingly the sympathetic tenderness which moves the heart at mention of Judaism, melting into a fellowship of sorrow on witnessing unwonted if not untimely physical sufferings, at length bursts forth in the burning tears of an outraged sense of justice and anon sinks down into ever-wakeful emotions of unutterable pity: for the ensuing anti-Christian persecution we behold, as a dismal proof of the utterly intolerant character of an emasculated Judaism. On the other side, the bolt once hurled, with what clearness and brilliancy appear as in an instant and shine forevermore the omnipotent energy and pervasive consolation of Christianity, that divine emanation which ever breathes in perfect unison a "woman behold thy son" with a "Father forgive them." Now, by these opposite influences, there is produced in the reader's mind a balance of feeling between pleasure and sadness; and this it is that gives, to a narrative which can sustain it, the charm of romance, without sacrificing in the least, but rather making penetrative the wholesome instructiveness of tangible truth.

That the ideal of such a work has not here been perfectly realized, gives (I think) credit directly to its candor and naturalness. Of incidental flaws I shall make no note, for of these you must be peculiarly sensible, being a sensible man. But I will admit, in anticipation of common consent, that there are, in your sometimes almost rustic depositions, many quickening passages which will interest to improve, and will especially awaken, it is hoped, a too dormant concern in behalf, not indeed of an ancestral religionism, yet of those infatuated by the anomaly of a fungus tenaciously adhering to the dead trunk of a once vigorous Judaism—a Judaism which, as pure, became when fulfilled nothing less than our expansive Christianity.

No heir under the New Testament is ignorant of his ultimate indebtedness to ancient Judaism. No Christian, having assumed this debt, can be indifferent to the religious movements and spiritual destiny of "Israel after the flesh." No mourner who earths over most precious clay of, alas, even impenitent dead, can yet feel such bitterness as he who, in giving sepulture, is pierced as by dagger point with the excruciating reflection, that *the fatal rejection of Messiah is made well nigh inevitable by a literal extinction of mental vision in the Jewish child.* Every youth therefore who has so much as a connection with Christian educators, will heartily thank God for this distinction, and then (we trust) bending with unfeigned pity over too clearly and sadly marked "olive branches," will do at least in prayer, what can be done thus if in no other way, for the deliverance of Israel from their worse than Arctic darkness.

God speed the day, when the branded, fugitive nation will receive the blood that speaketh better things than that of Abel, and antitypical Cain spring with incredible relief to recognize his renovated and messianic archetype in him, who is resembled by one more child of Abraham in the change which enabled him to say what the dialect of Targums is peculiarly strong in expressing—Be ye patterned by me precisely as I also indeed am by Messiah. And may your sincere effort subserve this desiderated result.

Yours and Israel's,

By the Holy Proselytism of Faith,

J. H. A.

New York City, May 21st, 1860.

PREFACE.

In presenting for your perusal a history of my youth and conversion from Judaism to Christianity, I expect to say but little with reference to the customs of my dear brethren, the Jews. Books are multiplied all over the world that impart the necessary information upon this subject. What little I may write will be directly or indirectly connected with my personal history.

The probability is in favor of this little book becoming a favorite of children both at home and in the precious Sabbath-school; consequently I have endeavored to simplify all my ideas to suit the capacity of the rising generation. I am aware however, that in this I am subjecting myself to wholesale criticism. Still, although I make no pretension to accuracy of style, much less to perfection, I venture to offer these humble pages to the intelligent reader also, believing that he will be sure to appreciate the motive at least that prompts me to obtrude myself upon his notice.

I am not ignorant of the fact that skeptics, garbed in both moral and religious habiliments, will be very apt to doubt the reality of some facts here related, particularly those having reference to the providential guidings of my Heavenly Father, and his singular care over me. Yet I know at the same time, that there are persons who love to doubt, and therefore will doubt, whatever the argument before them. Having learned to respect the common prejudices of the mass, I am not disposed to blame any one for professing to be ignorant of these things; but surely they are to blame who, being confessedly ignorant, themselves presume to judge the more enlightened. How true is that word of Revelation which declares that "The natural man receiveth not the things of the Spirit of God, for they are foolishness unto him; neither can he know them, because they are spiritually discerned: but he that is spiritual judgeth all things, yet he himself is judged of no man." 1 Cor. ii: 14. Pray with me then, dear reader, that this feeble effort may prove effectual in the hand of the Lord, shaking however slightly the kingdom of Satan, to the glory of God in Jesus Christ.

Perhaps you may be led to inquire what special object I have in writing these lines. I will try to satisfy you in few words. Having been a minister of the Gospel of Christ, for thirty years past, and knowing that I am growing old, can I do anything better, at this time of life, than to take up the Christian's watch-word, "The Jew, The Jew?" All Christendom is inquiring, "What is to become of the Jew?" Few indeed are the prayers that are offered for Israel's conversion to Christianity; while by far the more numerous petitions are sent up for their restoration to Jerusalem without any reference to their moral condition. Yet we do find an occasional Israelite who embraces the religion of the blessed Saviour and manifests a desire to take up his cross, and who naturally enough, becomes at once impatient to give public testimony in favor of this religion, which above all others he once most inveterately hated. Rarely however does the conversion of a Jew occur, without a consequent tale to be told of afflictions endured for the exercise of a free conscience. The natural result of suffering for Christ's sake is an experience of proportionate joy that buoys up his heart and overbalances his sorrows. And well does the Gentile Christian love to hear him tell of his peculiar joys and sorrows, losses and privations, and the not joyless tears called forth by persecutions, sacrifices and general anxieties that he has experienced for the cause of the precious Saviour. He *must* speak. He must extol *the* Name, that most glorious of all names which but a short time past he hated above all others. Thus the church of Christ feeds upon his discourse, as he talks about the Christian's warfare, from actual and vivid experience. The weak in faith gain strength, and the followers of Jesus universally thank God, and take courage. They see in the conversion of every such Jew, renewed, living evidence in favor of that religion upon which they are reposing all hope for salvation.

As inquisitiveness is an instinctive law of the human mind, no sooner is it known in any locality that a converted Jew is to preach " the unsearchable riches of Christ," than everybody becomes anxious to hear him, and hundreds do receive his testimony who otherwise would not hear the Gospel at all. Thus does the Lord Jehovah take " a worm to thresh a mountain," and so he makes " the wrath of man to praise him."

No wonder then that the Gentile Christian church feels encouraged, when she hears or reads the Jew's testimony in favor of the religion of the Messiah Jesus. Full well does she know with what implacable hatred the rigid Jew denounces the glorious Messiah—Jesus truly, though he was of Nazareth, aye because he had this very origin. Tenderly therefore does the church pity the scoffer, and deep down in her heart she evermore prays for the " Lopped off branch," knowing that, in the acqui-

sition of each converted Jew, there is at the same
time an additional, ten-fold evidence in favor of
Christianity. It uniformly rejoices the hearts of the
children of God to see numbers flocking around the
"Blood-stained banner of Immanuel," but when the
"mighty fall" and the enemy's ranks are thinned,
they still more rejoice at the prospect of enlarging
the boundaries of the conqueror's kingdom.

It was on a Tuesday evening, January the 7th,
A. D. 1834, that I received the holy ordinance of
Christian Baptism upon the profession of my faith
in Jesus Christ for eternal life. So that at the present writing (November, 1868,) it is nearly thirty-four
years since I "put on Christ." During this entire
period I have never ceased to declare and proclaim
to a perishing world "the unsearchable riches of
Christ."

In a short time after my baptism, I was constrained,
by stress of all my surroundings, to leave my native
country and find a new home where I could worship
my God with a free and unshackled conscience. My
steps were directed to the United States of America.
Here I have remained, preaching the Gospel of Christ.
Wherever I have been in this nation, I have found
different denominations of Christians to be of one
mind relative to my conversion. All such want to
know, and at once inquire, by what means I was led

to espouse the cause of the once hated, but now glorified Jesus. And when I have told them "what God has done for my soul," I have invariably been beset on every hand for a printed copy of my history. Many years ago, I gratified some by publishing one thousand small books; since then I have shrunk from complying with the growing number of similar requests, until now I have arrived at a stage of life when all the attending circumstances demand that, if I would leave this witness for Christ, I should, while I am in the vigor of my mind, record the same. I have resolved therefore to publish more fully my Auto-Biography, thus still "Preaching the kingdom of God and teaching those things which concern the Lord Jesus Christ with all confidence, no man forbidding."

I ask therefore of the reader charity for my imperfections, and of my God that he will cause this little book to redound to His own glory.

To my Jewish Kinsmen:

DEAR BRETHREN,—All my sympathies are with you. I take the liberty therefore of addressing you separately. From your infancy you have been taught to expect the Messiah. Times and seasons come and go; still you live—still are expectant. Rabbinical data have frequently held you, only for a short time however, then to vanish away and leave you still as fondly expectant. And notwithstanding the truth is obvious to your mind that the long, long expected Messiah of your fancy has not yet appeared, you live to-day no less expectant. What strange infatuation is this, my brethren, that seems to buoy you up so long against the agony of suspense? Nearly two thousand years have passed since the true Messiah dwelt among men, and you are still, still expectant. Why, with one consent, do you reject Jesus of Nazareth? Simply because your fathers continued to do so.

To what serious delusions have you consequently been exposed, at various periods of your history? Some of your pretended Messiahs, having been sustained by the rabbis, have appealed to the fortune of war to assert their "rights." They have all failed! And with no trifling damage, for the Romans will bear me witness that their successive failures occurred at the cost of *your* blood, of *your* liberty, of *your* holy fatherland.

But, I am not writing history for you. I desire to ask you, brethren, why do not your modern rabbis lead you to the light? Why do they act as a drowning man who grasps at straws? Why do they ex-

2

punge or explain away prominent prophecies that have any reference to the Messiah? They know that they cannot deceive you much longer. Though another "Barchochab, the son of the star," should again attempt to give the lie to Jesus of Nazareth, Jehovah would not leave you without an "Akiba" to reply, "the grass will spring from thy jaw-bone, and yet the 'Son of David' will not have come." The Almighty will never permit an impostor to prosper. How long then will it be, O Israel, before your long, long Expected will have come? Your rabbis have tried every expedient. They have endeavored to reconcile with the character of Messiah the names of very many of the old times saints. They tell you, at length, that nobody knows anything about it. Still, you seek for light. Who now shall give you the information you need? Can your rabbis? No: they who should be your leaders, alas, are very blind,—"they err, not knowing the scriptures." Let therefore the Prophets themselves speak to you the word of the living God. Then see if either of your pretended "great ones" answer to the character of "Messiah."

Dear brethren, I beseech you to be candid. Acknowledge your utter failure. Have you not had enough of rabbinical interpretations of the Targums, etc? Then why not, dear brethren, throw off your galling yoke? Jesus Christ it is who is the true and only Messiah. In him dwelt the fullness of the Godhead bodily. He is the Mediator between God and man. Remember also, dear brethren, that the times of this ignorance, God winked at, but now commandeth all men everywhere to repent, because he hath appointed a day in the which he will judge the world in righteousness by that Man whom he hath ordained, whereof he hath given assurance unto all men, in that he hath raised Him from the dead.

Receive then, dear reader, the word that is spoken for your good. Believe that as a Christian I live for your good. I preach Christ for your good. I write these lines for your good, your eternal good. O, do not longer harden your heart against Christianity. Do not longer reject the counsel of God against yourself. Remember, I pray you, that "It is appointed unto man once to die, and after that the Judgment." Are you ready? May the God of our fathers, of Abraham, Isaac, and Jacob, lead you to the light as it is in Jesus Christ. Amen.

JONAS ABRAHAM DAVIS.

AUTO-BIOGRAPHY.

CHAPTER I.

ABRAHAMIC DESCENT.

I was born of Jewish parents, in the city of London, England. This was also the land of my father's nativity. My grandfather on father's side was a German; and, if my recollection at this late date is correct, I would say that my great-grandfather was a Polander.

Readers as a general rule care nothing about tracing the pedigree of a stranger. Nor would I here obtrude my ancestry upon your notice, but for two interesting facts. The first is it proves that, in common with every true Jew, I have "Abraham to my father." The second and more noticeable consideration is that I am the only convert to Christianity ever known to have place in the whole line of this ancestry, on the side of either my father or mother. As a further proof of their far remove from the religion of the cross, I may cite the case of my great-grandfather, who was historied as a very remarkable man. He in particular was a very rigid Jew, and consequently an inveterate enemy to Christianity perhaps rendered more so by the fact of his being a rabbi, learned in the Targums, etc. He lived to be very old, dying in his one hundred and twelfth year, greatly lamented by his people. During his whole life, he had neither shears on his head, nor razor on his beard. His death however was sudden, coming on while he enjoyed the full possession of health and every faculty. So did he appear before the God of Abraham, the Giver of a greater Son, despised. When he was about one hundred years old, the Jews of London determined to make him their "Raaf" or chief rabbi. The language of his refusal is well worthy of note. "I have sins enough of my own to answer for, without taking upon myself the sins of my people." He died hating Jesus of Nazareth; and his Christless death strengthened the mountain of animosity against the "Lord's anointed" in his posterity. But, glory be to the great Jehovah, who selected me from among them, and made me a living monument of His signal grace and mercy—me, the direct offspring of this anti-Christian sire.

CHAPTER II.

Writing about myself at this period of my life, I am like a man who having passed safely over a very dangerous road in the dark, calmly sits down in broad day-light to contemplate the journey. He goes over every minutiæ with equal interest, simply because they were all on the road over which he has passed unharmed. The few bruises that he has received by no means disqualify him for the business of the day. Yet he has them, acting out their part in his moral nature, serving him as faithful mementoes of the past, and at the same time admonishing him to exercise more caution in the future. How futile would be the effort of one who has never encountered similar dangers, to make this traveler believe that what he relates of his journey is visionary, a mere whim. He would simply reply, "I *know* it to be so, I have been there; I'm bruised, and I feel grateful that I am not injured more." How completely analogous to this is the real journey of a Christian. I find it to be true in my own case; and as the leadings of the divine hand are the same toward every true child of grace, I am the more emboldened in my endeavor to gather together the materials that proved to be of such incalculable value in moulding my mind into what it has been so many years of my unworthy life. Many are the links necessary to the existence of one chain. Even so, when an experienced Christian would glorify God by a narration of his experience in the journey of life, when he would stand up boldly before the followers of Jesus, and call to them as David did in Psalm lxvi. 16 : " Come and hear all ye that fear God, and I will declare what He hath done for my soul,"—then can he look at the smallest event of his life, and find in it something that makes a valuable contribution to his narrative of gracious facts. Thus he will glorify God in his body and his soul. And this is what I now intend to do.

My whole life has been attended by some afflictive providence. Inheriting a small and feeble body from my mother, I must have been but poorly prepared to grapple with the sad adversities which commenced their ravages upon me at or about my fourth year. Scarlet fever, the common enemy of childhood, threatened to cast me into the jaws of death. To my grave will I carry with me evidence of the severity of a relapse. The existence of several scars suffice as reminders to me, yet stand not alone, the suffering they indicate not being enough to answer the purpose of my Heavenly Father. When at length I was able to leave my bed, it was discovered that I was entirely deaf. Internal ulcers had formed, leaving me down to this time with unsound ears and very little power of hearing. Continued and aggravating sicknesses still preyed upon my feeble frame, until I was almost past recovery.

While this state of things continued with me, it was agreed on all hands, that a *dead saint*, for a time of affliction, is no less essential than a little medical science. As a last resort, therefore, I must be carried to the synagogue, that I might have the blessing of the chief rabbi in my behalf. The name of some one of the Old Scripture saints must be conferred upon me. So "Abraham" was added to my name —which certainly benefitted me, nominally at least. Doubtless I was very innocent when my "eighth" day arrived, that day for the administration of the rite of circumcision. I had then been labelled Jonas, or Jonah, that is to say, "a dove." Now they are giving a middle name, Abraham, to be translated "father of many nations." These, added to my dear father's name—Davis, probably Davids, a corruption of David, that is to say, "beloved"—afford me a chain of names certainly most euphoniously linked together: Beloved and dove-like father of many nations. The ceremony is ended; and the condition of things stands something like this: Father foots the bill; he is somewhat poorer for that. I have a "blessing" and a new name. None the richer am I for this. In the providence of God I regain a little health, still am very deaf. So Father Abraham is extolled for my restored health, and Doctor Kish is blamed for the continued deafness.

A short time after my restoration to health, I met with an accident, which well nigh proved fatal. One day, while at play with my elder brother, I fell, breaking both my arms. This accident laid me low again for a very long time. But out of this also the Lord delivered me, and for a few months my afflicted childhood moved on undisturbed by any new calamity. Little did I dream, however, that there was a sorrow in store for me which childhood may outlive, but can never, never feel reconciled to.

The health of my precious mother failed. I did not then understand what it meant. But when I knew that mother was preparing to leave home for a little season, I began to comprehend that my own mother was really, seriously sick. And soon it pleased my Heavenly Father to deprive me of her. Well do I remember climbing upon that lovely mother's knee. Vividly in memory revives the pale countenance that gazed at me through streaming tears; tangible to my perception, even now, is that embrace which pressed me to a truly maternal bosom; and to this day do I remember her last hug, her last kiss, and that last piece of cake which she gave me, as she took leave of us all, for a journey to Manchester. I recall to my mind's eye how tardily she stepped toward the parlor door, at which she had scarcely arrived when she turned back again to the window where I was sitting, playing with my piece of cake. All that can be called *mother*, flowed from her soul. She kissed me again and again. "Be a good boy," said she, "mamma will soon come back." Not so, alas! she did not soon come back; I saw her no more. She died in Manchester about three weeks after she arrived there. Her ruling passion too was strong in death. She made but one dying request of my father. "Take care of Jonas," was its burden. She left five children, I being the youngest. In a few days, my heart-broken father returned without my dear mother. It was only then that I fairly realized that mother, my mother was dead, actually dead. After all, now it was that I began to understand what it is to be afflicted.

This providential stroke was enough for me. I was now without my mother when not more than six or seven years old and withal exceedingly puny. Heavy stroke! But alas, that she died in the Jewish faith, rejecting the Messiah. Still, revered be her name for her genuine virtues. If my holy religion permitted me to offer to Almighty God but one prayer during the whole course of my life-time, for the benefit of the departed, that prayer should be, God save my mother doubly dead, yet one whose memory ever lives as that of mother.

But there is no repentance in the grave, though after it the pious heart twice smitten may find healing. My grandmother now took charge of the family, while struggling in addition against the infirmities of age.

A few weeks after my mother was buried, I met with still another accident which nearly cost me life. A large bathing tub in the cellar kitchen had just been in use by one of the family who left it standing nearly full of water. Walking near it, I saw a piece of bread floating on the water. My venturesomeness at once prompted me to try obtain it, and while endeavoring to do so, the chair on which I stood, no longer backing the effort, slipped away letting me down into the water. And thus I should probably have been drowned but for the timely help of my infirm grandmother, who fancying that she heard a very unusual noise below, came tottering down as speedily as she could and dragged me out half dead. In the moment of excitement, she tore off my wet clothes, and this being cleverly done, she raised a most spanking breeze, in the shape of a sound drubbing, before I had sufficiently recovered to know whether I was dead or alive. The discipline, however, seemed an evidence of my good old grandmother's knowledge of " cause and effect." But whether she was a philosopher or not, one thing is certain; the process she employed had two *marked* effects upon me, the first being physical, and the second metaphysical, so moralizing its subject that ever since that notable event, with its exclamation marks, I have hated the sight of a bathing tub.—But let not this reflect upon a religion that magnified ablutions.

Thus far in life, God was my Preserver, and I knew it not. He was even then overruling my life for future use. He saved me from the plague. He delivered me from danger. He cast me down, and raised me up. And although I carry with me the mark of his afflictive providence, yet I can sing, in spirit and in truth—

"When in the slippery paths of youth,
With heedless steps I ran,
Thine arm unseen conveyed me safe,
And led me up to man."

CHAPTER III.

SCHOOL EXPERIENCES.

Some time before the tears for the loss of my mother were all shed, even in the short space of about ten months, my father married again. The Jewess whom he brought home, was a lady of surpassing beauty. She was only thirty years of age, being but one year older than my eldest sister. No longer were we a happy family. On the contrary, a dark veiling was now visible on the countenance of every member of the family; misty gloom took possession of each heart. We were not sad because another occupied the place at father's side, but because she was not mother. And when my dear old grandmother so reluctantly resigned the government of the family to her to whom of right it now belonged, and retired to her own private room, the pent-up sighs which for several days past had been struggling, and only groaning, mother!—all now burst through the barriers, and with loud lamentations and tears, I alone entered the room with grandmother, and laid my head upon her lap in grief inconsolable. From that hour until I was sent away to school, I was her constant companion. But I will speak of her more fully in due time.

My step-mother did the best she could, but she

was inexperienced, and so in wide contrast to "mother." This circumstance, together with the increasing infirmities of grandmother, daily led me to feel more keenly than ever the loss of my parent. My oldest brother having died a short time previous, but four of us remained, two sisters and one brother. They did not suffer as I did, they were much older, were not afflicted, and therefore could help themselves. They soon became reconciled to the change of base, and launched out into the gay world with more splendor than ever, my father and step-mother leading the way. It was not long therefore before my uncombed, parasitical hair exhibited unmistakable signs of neglect.

Although I was yet very young, my father saw that it was necessary to send me away from home. But where should he send me? It was soon decided that I must go to boarding-school. Preparations were immediately made for a speedy disposal of me, and without delay carried into effect. I have even now some recollection as to the character of the romantic aspirations that took fast hold of my boyish spirit. Sad as I felt at the idea of leaving grandmother, I could not resist the pleasurable excitement there was in the prospect of going to school, so far away it was, *ten miles* from home! Where is the boy to be found who would not yell for very joy while under the operation of soap, water, towels, combs, etc., and then the donning of an entire new suit of fustian, (the storing of an entire new outfit being additional—a whole trunk full,) that he might have an old-fashioned stage ride, and above all, go

away so very far, ten long, long miles? My dear
Yankee-boy reader, who lives on wonders, and travels
by steam thirty miles an hour, can't see any fun in a
ten-mile stage ride. Neither can I *now*. But I saw
it then; and yell I did, from the very start until I
fairly arrived at my school destination.

Will my reader have any charity for me when I
relate that the instant the stage stopped at the gate
where I was to enter, my vociferous talking stopped,
my romance vanished and my aerial castles subsided
into an unspeakable gloom? Yes, involuntarily I
shrank from entering. I wanted to go home again;
I wanted to see grandma; I didn't want to go to
school. But crying was of no avail; my trunk was
carried in, while I was coaxed in. Finding myself
in for it, I resolved to make the best of the event,
and in I went with as good grace as I could possibly
command. The school was in character purely Jewish. The principal was Rabbi Mosha Eleazer Solomon, and his assistants were his two sons, Zalmor
and Shemuile. The location was Brixton, in sight
of the world-renowned tread-mill. My teachers were
certainly learned men, especially in that department
of Jewish literature, so essential in an Israelite.
Their school had the reputation of being the best of
the kind that England could afford. Doubtless it
was unsurpassed. But it had no seasoning from the
salt of the Gospel of Jesus. Restraining grace ruled
not there. The teachers were in their lives licentious, and openly profane in the very presence of the
pupils. But as was prophesied, "there shall be like
people like priest;" and thus by common consent

all here was pronounced "very good." By experience I learned, moreover, that "being in Rome, I must do as do the Romans." Very soon, therefore, I took on enough of Brixton's *polite literature* (?) to initiate me into the brave (?) accomplishment (?) of swearing as manfully (?) as my proficient teachers.

Doubtless the reader will readily understand that all the religious influences which had heretofore been thrown around me, were directly calculated to hold me firmly to the religion of my fathers. True, I had not learned to *love* Judaism, but possessing a temperament susceptible of religious influences, and knowing nothing but "Moses and the Prophets," it was not a hard matter for me to shut out everything else, when I was shut off from it. And so it came to pass that at this school I learned to *hate* "Jesus of Nazareth." Many times during my days of childhood, I had heard that name coupled with stories, ridiculous, licentious, and blasphemous. And I verily believed all that my dear grandma told me was true. My juvenile prejudices thus became established, for the one and against the other. But now it was that I learned positively to hate. It must be borne in mind, that whatever else a Jewish boy studies, whatever accomplishments he may aspire to, he *must* have a good Hebrew education. This is absolutely essential to his religion. In truth, this noble language belongs to the Jew, all over the world. Having had a fair start at home in the study of both Hebrew and English, and possessing withal a disposition to acquire an education, I soon entered into the spirit of the daily round of school duties. At this school I

learned that if I would be a *good* Jew, I *must* hate
" Jesus of Nazareth." I would not for a moment
have the reader think that studying the Hebrew
necessarily imparts prejudice. No: but studying it
in a Jewish school has this effect. Fortunes too are
expended in acquiring Talmudical fables and Hebrew
nonsense, which, if dispensed with, would retard
Judaism, and frustrate its own purpose of hurting
Christianity.

Few persons (outside of the Jewish family) are
aware of the great disadvantage under which a Jewish boy in England labors in acquiring an education.
This is owing to the fact that there is so much mean-
ingless religion crowded into the brain of the youthful
tyro, and swallow it he must, even under penalty.
No regard is paid to his capacity in this respect.
Here, he has no election. Here, he must learn that
his Gentile neighbor is a doomed man. Here, he is
instructed to retort upon every Gentile, " I will not
eat, drink, or pray with you." No religious instruction is imparted to the Jewish youth, unless it is
blended with something that is prejudicial to the
character of Christ. In a Jewish school everybody
hates " Jesus of Nazareth." They speak of him de-
risively as " The *Christian's* God." This abuse again
is supported by ten thousand fables represented as
being founded upon the Talmud; for the ears of the
learner are constantly assailed by strange words, such
as, " Masora," " Talmud," " Mischna," " Gemara,"
all purporting to be correct exponents, either of the
sacred text, or of the traditional addenda, the rabbins alone forming the tribunal in every case.

3

After all is said that can be, to detract from the dignity and truthfulness of the Christian religion, another great mistake is made in attempting to cramp the expanding mind. The brains of youth will exercise their natural function. Many a time while sitting in class, listening to Rabbi Mosha tell some old, dried up, traditional yarn, have I seen a well-known, mischievous snap of the eye pass around from one to another. Rabbi Mosha always construed the satirical smile of his class, as an expression of approbation. So finally the young "free thinkers," feeling safe in playing the ruse, would be tempted to give free vent, and laugh outright. Sometimes, however, we would be caught in our own trap. The rabbi didn't want that boy to laugh just then; and well would the poor fellow pay for his fun. It not unfrequently happened after one or other of us had received the benefit of a stiff rattan, that with smarting shoulders and back we would sulkily enter the play ground at recess to be instantly surrounded by a score of sympathisers. No tears would be shed, but with stoical heroism the sufferer would patiently await as his relief a chance to ease his own conscience. This chance was found in the play ground, and on this wise : "I say, boys, what did you think of *that* —wasn't it a whopper?" "Yes," speaks up Ike, "worse than that, 'twas a downright lie." "I wonder," chimes in Abe, "if old Mosha thinks that we are a-goin' to swaller all that stuff?"

Somebody then swears a round oath, and so that rattan is doomed to be split before night.

It is not uncommon to see a number of the boys

in groups, amusing each other with an *original* story that one of the number somewhere had heard that somebody had told somewhere about the Christians. Here *somebody* breaks in with, "That's a lie." "True as the Gemara; ask old Mosha if it *aint*." Nothing daunted, each boy tries to shoot higher than his fellow, and many a boyish tale is told, founded—*of course*—upon rabbinical infallibility. But hark, the school-bell rings. "Run, boys, run," and running speeches keep pace. The last one is—"Jose, keep your face straight, this time"

CHAPTER IV.

A GROWTH OF PREJUDICES.

I shall doubtless find it necessary to refer to my school days again, in another part of my history. Having written enough for one short division, I presume that it will meet with the approbation of my patient reader if I, for the time being, change the subject.

The Indian's idea of the gravitation of the earth is not more absurd than the Jew's idea of the relation which the whole human family sustain to their God. An East Indian was once asked why the world does not fall? He replied, "Because it stands on the back of a large elephant." "But what does the elephant stand on?" He replied, "On a large turtle." "But what does the turtle stand on?" He briefly replied, "Mud."

Early in life I was made to believe that there exists but one grand division of the family of man; and that it is, between the Jews and the Christians. So whoever is not of blood relation to Abraham, is a Christian, and unless he submits to the right of circumcision and observes the so-called law of Moses, he cannot be saved. The Jew thus makes no difference between Christians and Heathen. It is enough for him to know that you are not a Jew. This alone, in his belief, will result in the loss of your soul.

Christianity teaches a doctrine just as discriminating, namely: "There is no other name under heaven given among men whereby we must be saved," but the name of Jesus. Believing this, the Christian heart agonizes for the conversion of the Jew. Although I was at this time entirely ignorant, aye in total darkness concerning all that pertains to Christianity, yet sometimes a query arose in my mind as to what would become of all the people in the world who were not Jews. I never knew a Jew to utter one word of sympathy in behalf of all these lost, lost Christians: I experienced none. I have heard the rabbins even exult at the idea that there is no salvation for any but Jews. In this sentiment my own heart participated, for I never knew what sympathy for my fellow-man, as man, could mean, until my imprisoned sensibilities were set at liberty, when I received the ever-blessed Jesus as my own Saviour.

No impressions are so hard to overcome as those with which we have been brought up. Prejudice from education is the chief cause of all the errors in existence. But in such a system as this, out of which, by the grace of God, I have been delivered, there is not even the show of a chance for the youthful mind to arrive at the truth, when it would embrace it. If at any time a Jewish youth should inquire, "who is this Christian's God about whom I hear so much talk?" he will receive but one character of reply—"'Jesus of Nazareth,' the crucified one, the impostor, the bastard, the evil angel," etc.

If an unsatisfied mind should still excite his inquisitive propensity, he will in all probability be amused with some rabbinical nonsense, such as I have been enlightened with. For example—"Once upon a time our fathers had a beautiful temple. They had in it a beautiful organ. 'Jesus of Nazareth' stole it away and gave it to his followers; and for this crime the Jews caught him and hanged him. This Jesus, my darling, he is the God of the Christians."

What if the intelligent American Jew discards this stupid stuff? What if it is an old woman's yarn? What if the more enlightened Jewish reader feels ashamed to be in company with such flimsy, linsey-woolsey talk? Is it more insipid than volumes of similar Talmudical infallibilities? What if you reject even them? Is it not, after all, the very material that holds Judaism together? Certainly it is so: and behold the proof when you are told that the ridiculous stuff which I have mentioned above, is believed by the old people among foreign Jews to this day, who, in order to show their hatred for everything that they suppose to be in any way connected with Christianity, actually stop up their ears with their fingers when they have to pass a church on "Sunday," through fear of receiving contamination by hearing the sound of the organ.

Jews further charge Christians with worshiping the cross upon which Christ was fastened. They spurn the idea that God should manifest himself as —a son. No; say they, "If there is *one* relation, there must be a *chain* of them." Now, it would ill become the nature of this book for me to attempt to sustain by Revelation the divinity of Christ; but what can I do else than deplore the blindness of my brother who is ignorant of every description of religion except the Judaism that has been crowded together by rabbinical pressure into his unenlightened mind. For the rabbins are the exclusive disposers of the creed for the people, who *must* believe everything that is taught, whereas nothing is taught but what is best calculated to keep the mass in perpetual darkness. As a result it is found that these professed worshipers of the only true God, are, in respect to Messianic prophecy, entirely ignorant of their own scriptures.

O! my God, remove, I beseech thee, the gross darkness from my dear, but deluded people. Well did the "Prince of Peace" pronounce the rabbins to be "blind leaders of the blind." Blessed Lord, save them from "falling into the pit together."

A common error exists among Christians, which leads them into a false sympathy for the Jew. It grows out of the apparent *zeal* of my people in their worship, on account of which they are supposed to stand a good chance for salvation. Every professing Christian ought to know better than to submit such a momentous question to a game of chance. Alas! zeal is not religion, especially when it is exercised in a cause so bad as to shut out light, when it seems to be imploring for admittance. But now the Gentile reader may wonder again how the once chosen people can remain so ignorant of the Gospel in a Christian land, where so much light is shining around them. The difficulty at once vanishes when we behold in them the truth of our blessed Redeemer's words, "Every one that doeth evil hateth the light, neither cometh to the light, lest his deeds should be reproved." This is true of "every one," Gentile as well as Jew.

Still, making every allowance, it is matter for astonishment to see with what skilful tact the Jew evades every prophetic scripture that has any bearing upon the Messiah. From infancy taught to reject the blessed Jesus, he consequently imbibes an early hatred. This grows with him, it gains strength with him, and so becomes a component part of him. He hates, because his father hated; he says the same words that his father said, and he uses the same prayer-book, simply because the rabbins require it.

Such is the position that I occupied with reference to the Christian religion, during the morning of my days. This is the "horrible pit" out of which the Lord plucked me. And glory forever be to His holy name, He hath set me in a clean place.

I remember to have once read of two wicked men who tried to excel each other in fabricating a falsehood. The first said that "he had actually reached the moon by ascending a tall ladder, and that he drove a ten-penny nail clear through it." "I know that to be a truth," replied the other, "it's no lie at all; for, while you were fixing your ladder, I was behind the moon, and when you drove your nail through, I clinched it."

The lofty moral standard of the popular literature of the world to-day, certainly excels everything of which ancient seers ever dreamed. So the above fable can only be excelled by a modern relation of a fact, true as conjectures on the weather. "Bill was a notorious liar. Tom, meeting him one day, accosted him with, 'Bill, tell the biggest lie you ever told, and I'll stand treat.' Bill looked quite surprised, and appeared to feel insulted. 'Why,' said he, 'I never told a lie in all my life.' '*Take* my cap,' quoth Tom, 'I'll stand the treat.' "

Corresponding departures from existing fact, and equally extravagant, are the refuges to which the rabbins resort in order to evade the force of the prophetical words which they are obliged to read. One example must suffice.

The Patriarch Jacob on his death-bed predicted, Genesis xlix. 10: "The sceptre shall not depart from Judah, nor a lawgiver from between his feet, until *Shiloh* come, and unto *him* shall the gathering, or obedience, of the people be." Early in life I made many inquiries of my instructors as to what all this meant. Every question received in reply a different evasion. Nobody knew anything about "Shiloh." He was Solomon, Artaxerxes, Moses, Napoleon; he had been, he would never come; a truth, a fiction; a man of some sort, a myth;—doctors disagreed; learned rabbins did not know.

But existing facts everybody, and so I, must know. True, I did not understand anything about "Shiloh," but I did know, and every Jew knows, that "the sceptre" *has* "departed from Judah," and that "the lawgiver" has "passed from between his feet." This alone should be received as evidence that "Shiloh" has indeed come.

Yet a crafty priesthood can evade even this. "Shiloh," they say, "has not come, and it can be proved by—Rabbi Gerson. Now a learned rabbi is entitled to a fair hearing. He shall have it; and it is to be hoped that he will not enlighten Israel by a man-in-the-moon story. Hear him! In his book, "Geliloth Eretz," the rabbi affirms, with an oath, that he will not lie in a single letter, but will relate what he himself has seen. He then says that in his travels he found a river sixteen miles in breadth, each mile being eight thousand feet long, and the river thus twenty-four English miles wide. The water of this river flows with such rapidity that the sound thereof is heard at a distance of two days' journey. The river is called Sabbatyon, or Sambatyon, because it throws up large stones as high as a house all the week long; yet it rests and becomes perfectly dry two hours before the commencement of the Sabbath, beginning again to run with all its fury as soon as Sabbath is ended. Beyond this river, he continues, there are many Jews, even as the sand of the sea, living too in great affluence and plenty. They have twenty-four kings and a powerful king is over the whole. He is Shiloh.

My reader may arrive at a just conclusion about Rabbi Gerson; but he is at least bound to admit that he outdoes the man behind the moon.

The licentiousness of a corrupt priesthood made a very injurious impression upon my mind, yet I did not dare to doubt their word in matters of religion. No Jew can appeal from the decision of the "Chief Rabbi," however immoral his life may be. Every

difficult question is referred to his infallibility.   And
some of these "difficult" questions are so childish
that a squeaking doll might almost hoot at them.
His omniscience decides all disputes, levies taxes,
imposes fines, pronounces penances, prays for the
dead, and usurps power over a kind of purgatory.

In consequence of these manifest corruptions, I
was in a great measure shaken in my affection towards the Jewish priesthood.   But nothing had so
strong a tendency to unsettle my confidence in them,
as one circumstance of which I will speak in the
next division of my history.

CHAPTER V.

DEATH'S SECOND KNOCKING.

I have now arrived at the close of a period which has covered two years and a half of my boarding-school life. In the proper place, I expect again to recur to this school. I had been home four times since I entered it, the vacations being but two during the year, namely, in the spring, for the Passover festival, and at Autumn, for the Atonement fast. In some respects these days of schooling were really pleasant. Part of the time I had the companionship of my elder brother; and I was made happy by frequent visits from my dear father also. Many times during the school session, the old lumbering stage would stop at our gate and disburden itself of certain packages of extras, all fresh from the hands of excellent Jewish cooks. This consideration, always timely and very welcome, had a tendency to reconcile me to my daily fare. We used to say over a Hebrew thanksgiving at every meal time, and always repeated the same words whether our bread was mouldy or not, whether there was enough or not, (and generally it was the *not*.) A more appropriate " blessing," likewise worded always the same, which I learned in after years, had I then known, I should certainly have suggested to the boys, that it might have displaced the Hebrew, pro. tem. For the more special occasions, a crisp, common sense English stanza would have been a good substitute:

> Before we eat,
> Let us entreat
> The Lord, to bless
> Our *scanty* mess."

Indeed it was a great relief to my conscience, when a parcel from home was put into my hands. At such times, I used to think that my step-mother was not so unkind after all. But when I recognized something, as I thought, from the hands of good old grandma, not a hungry chap within the sound of the smacking of my lips *dare* ask for a single mouthful.

These stage stoppages were so frequent that scarcely a day passed without leaving a home memento for one or another of the boys. All postal communications, however, were forbidden, except in cases of emergency. Such an emergency was now at hand. A letter arrived. I must go home quickly, grandma lies very sick: she is dying. I did not now exult at the prospect of going home. In muteness I entered the coach; silently I traveled along. I re-entered my home (?) in deepest gloom, and with sorrow grown fearful, I saw her die! She knew me, and beckoned me to come near her bed. She would have spoken to me, but my deafness admonished her. Long and steadily she gazed upon me. I saw her speaking, but I could not hear a word. My heart was bursting. O! that I *could* hear her! I leaned over her. Her lips still moved, but now in silence. I drew a step back and looked at her through my tears. I could do nothing more.

The nurse had been looking on this scene in silence, but presently she exclaimed, "Poor soul!" Whether the exclamation was meant for me or my dying grand-parent I do not know. But grandma heard it and took it to herself. In an instant, summoning all her remaining strength to help her, she replied in quite a strong voice, "My soul is not poor, *aint* I a daughter of Israel?" She never spoke again. In her ninety-fifth year she left this world.

Many and tedious are the ceremonies before and at the interment of the dead. And if I indulge my pen at this writing, I shall multiply these pages beyond my calculation.

Preparations for interment are always rapidly completed. Before the coffin (which is uniformly quite plain) is taken from the house, the entire family of the deceased are required to stand on one side of it. The clerk of the synagogue takes his place on the other side. Now follows the ceremony of each one in turn leaning over the corpse. This however is sometimes dispensed with. The clerk then makes a slit with a knife on the right side of the outside garment, and he tears down a strip about two inches long. Misery and rags are an emblem of grief.

The female members of the family seldom or never attend a funeral. So that mournful duty devolved upon my father, brother, and me. According to custom, the corpse was carried to the Charnel-house to *receive* prayers before interment. Now followed the ceremony of walking seven times around the dead. Afterward, when the corpse arrives at the grave, it is set down over the opening,

while the officiating rabbi, facing the East, says a
solemn prayer for the dead.   Of course the rabbi has
a right to a fee for his services, and every Jew right-
fully expects to pay it !   The regular fee was half of
a crown, or two shillings and sixpence, or five York
shillings, or (if you can better understand this) sixty-
two and a half cents.   As to the payment of this fee,
my father had arranged with my elder brother to
hand it to the rabbi at the grave-side when a certain
point of the ceremony should be reached.

It was the first funeral I had ever attended, and
never in my life had I felt the pangs of sorrow so
keenly as upon this occasion.   My mother dead !
My grandmother dead !   Alas, " they left the world
to sorrow and to me."   Somehow the weeping became general, all for one, poor, old woman.   So-
lemnity was seated upon every heart, and sorrow
upon every brow.   There stood the officiating rabbi
at the head of the coffin, and our position was at the
right side.   In awful silence we stood and gazed
while another prayer was being offered to Almighty
God for the soul of the dead.   Whether my brother
forgot that he held the rabbi's fee, or whether he
was solemnly absorbed in thought, certain it is, that
he was not up to time; for suddenly the rabbi opened
his hypocritical eyes, and turning nervously toward
my brother, he extended the open left hand towards
him, while, without stopping a second in his prayer,
he tapped the open palm with the index finger of
his right hand several times in rapid succession,
muttering at each tap, with greedy gaze, " tip, tip,
tip."   My frightened brother was startled.   I

watched all these movements with boyish leer, wondering what was up. In a moment my brother took the hint, and offered him his fee, which he no sooner saw, than he grabbed it in a hurry. In the twinkling of an eye it was buried, with no funeral service, down deep in his capacious pocket.

Where is the boy, who is a boy, that could have maintained his gravity in the presence of such a farce? I could not. This was a little too much for me, and in spite of all my effort to restrain, I buried my face in my handkerchief, held in both hands, and was actually convulsed with laughter. Reaction had taken place, so this overcame me. I could not hold my unnerved body still. I laughed until I actually cried. Then the general and abiding impression that I was crying became again correct. My brother, meanwhile, was no better off than myself. He had caught the spark, and was already bursting to find vent. I laid my head upon brother's shoulder, and squeaked, "tip, tip, tip." This was altogether more than he could bear. In a moment he too had his face buried, laughing most cruelly. Not being able to keep our feet any longer, we retired to a distance to have our laugh out, in a sitting posture. "Tip, tip, tip," muttered my brother. That was enough for our purpose; we laughed together until we were exhausted, and glad we were when the prayers for the dead were exhausted too.

Our company of mourners, however, mistaking our merriment for broken-hearted grief, united with us, as they supposed, in loud accents of sorrow for the departed. When all was over, and we were led to calm reflection, O! how we censured ourselves for this conduct. Still in our hearts we said, "May our sin rest upon that half-shaved priest." Years have now passed away. I have lived many of these with the love of Jesus in my heart, and have preached salvation through Him to thousands of my fellow creatures, pointing them to the great truth that Jesus Christ "hath brought life and immortality to light through the Gospel." I think of the grandmother we laid away at that time, of my mother who went before, and of my father who followed a while later. They all died hating Jesus! Is blood from Abraham enough for eternity? Can aught that descends from the Patriarch invalidate the breathing of the Prophet—"The child shall die a hundred years old; but the sinner, being a hundred years old, shall be accursed?"

4

CHAPTER VI.

BRIXTON AGAIN.—PORK AND HYPOCRISY.

A few days after the funeral, I was doomed to return again to my school at Brixton. So great a change in my feelings had taken place, that had I been sentenced to the cruel "tread mill" to finish out my time, I could not have gone into it more reluctantly. I resumed my studies with a heavy heart, and the recollection of the past often drew a private tear from my eyes. My prejudice was excited against my preceptors in consequence of the conduct of the rabbi at the funeral. Had I had control of myself at that time, I never should have submitted to be instructed again by a Jew. But it was vain to attempt rebellion against my father's wish for me to continue at that school. Study hard I did: I liked that. But several weeks passed finding me, one after the other, with a heavy heart. Every fresh talmudical anecdote that my teacher would amuse us with, served only to increase my dislike for them. One feature alone I did like: I acquired in these, material wherewith to persecute the hated Christians.

The reader is doubtless in the dark as to any knowledge of the weight attached to rabbinical teaching—a teaching which is always prejudicial to the character of Christianity, if not in one way, in

another. While I was under that immediate influence, hearing only one side of the question, all their
arguments, lop-sided as they are, appeared to be of
magnitude. But since I, " by the grace of God,"
have been permitted to measure my ground by the
glorious Gospel of Christ, all their arguments flee
before it as mere ephemeral shadows, and sink as
arguments into utter imperceptibility.

The Christian community, as a general thing, are
ignorant of the amount of prejudice an inquiring
Jew has to contend with, and the difficulties he has
to surmount, ere he can openly espouse the cause of
Christ. Some of his barriers which are apparently
insignificant are oftimes the most insurmountable.
We will speak, for instance, of the Jew's objection
to eating swine flesh. In after years, when I had
surmounted every other objection against Christianity, lo, the·poor, inoffensive hog alone remained
in my way. This may be accounted for by the deep-
rooted prejudice I imbibed against hogs and Christians alike, at school. Swine are refused by the
Jews, as an article for food, on two accounts. First,
because their meat was expressly forbidden, in common with certain other animals pronounced by Jehovah to be unclean, (see Leviticus xi: 7–8.) That,
therefore, is to them argument enough. Secondly,
the porker has been used by Pagans as a weapon of
persecution against them. It is, therefore, the more
abominable. The Jew, therefore, as a Jew, does
right in refusing the flesh of swine. And an almost
insurmountable objection against Christians is founded upon their eating it. Blessed be the Lord for the

removal of every legal yoke in Christ Jesus, whose
glorious Gospel teaches "what God hath cleansed,
that call not thou common."

Consistency with what one professes is a virtue.
Young as I was, I could not help noticing the glaring inconsistencies that stalked abroad at noon-day,
among my people. Some of these contributed
largely to shake my faith in Judaism. The mention of but one novel circumstance, must sufficiently
illustrate this point.

By the date now reached, several years of my
school life were gone forever. Hitherto my life had
been dragged along without variation or recreation.
It had been customary for my father to leave the
city every summer with some of the family, and
spend some time on the sea-coast. This summer
father resolved to take me along. The party consisted of my father, step-mother, two sisters, and my
poor, little self; afterwards we were joined by a Gentile lady friend. Now we are fairly under way, with
steam up, spirits ditto, hearts light, purses heavy,
bound for Margate, for a summer's excursion. It
was seventy-two miles from London, across salt water. This time, at least, I realized more truth than
poetry in the matter, for it was not long before sea-
sickness stiffened me out. I really felt as though I
was being rowed up the fabled salt river in reality.
However, all the company participated; father too,
although he had left his counting-room and come
away for recreation, could not help casting up other
"accounts" where there was more "room" for
them. It really did me good to see their faces as

woe-begone as my own. But never mind the little
unpleasantness, cheer up; we have safely arrived at
Margate.

Cessation from study, recreation, change of scene
and of air, with the unpatented, yet availing *pana-
cea*, sea-sickness, all combined to operate like magic
upon my general health. I left my bed at sun-rise,
and bathed in the sea before breakfast. During the
day, I walked along the beach, examining curious
shells and such geological and maritime substances
as the sea would wash ashore. Thus each day I
improved my opportunity, at the same time acquiring considerable educational light, much to the
benefit of my health as well. We took our meals
only four times a day, namely, breakfast, dinner, tea,
and lastly, supper. A few nick-nacks, or something
harder, affectionately received " ad interim," filled
up the measure of our daily necessary and unneces-
sary requirements. But I was a growing boy then,
and *of course* always had a good appetite. Eating
times followed each other in such rapid succession,
that I found no time to have God "in all my
thoughts." I didn't even think of Rabbi Gerson's
"big river." One day, after a forenoon spent as
usual, "up to time" in all its appointments, I walked
home for dinner, and being, notwithstanding, exceedingly hungry, I became rather ill-humored. At last
the savory fragrance of the highly seasoned dishes
reached my olfactories, and contributed much towards strengthening my hope as the servants set
these eatables safely or unsafely upon the table.
We observed the usual ceremony of *washing hands*

before eating; and at the table, prayers were duly said. I confess I was pleased with this feature so consistent, especially as I noticed that Mrs. B., a Gentile lady, was one of our company. At a signal, the covers were instantly removed from off the dishes, which without reluctance exhibited the concealed treasures. One dish particularly attracted my attention. Whew, earth, air and fire, water and steam! "what's that?" My surprise was soon dissipated by father's scientific carving of the beautiful stranger. The preference of dishes was given to the company, and each voted to treat the stranger with common politeness, and cultivate an *intimate* acquaintance. Of course, I followed suit. I assure you, polite reader, that we did not mince the matter at all. We all went to work as if we were used to it, for by the time we had finished operating upon the mysterious visitor, there was but a very small piece left on the dish, and this only for good manner's sake. Dessert over, we returned thanks, in the form of which occur these words: "When thou hast eaten and art satisfied, then thou shalt bless the Lord thy God." In truth we were this time all quite satisfied—but, as usual, what next? We now left the table, each to spend the afternoon as easily as possible until tea-time. So letting others do as they chose, I, like a lonely sheep, strolled off to the sea-shore, where I amused myself in searching for natural curiosities. I had been some time at my favorite solitary amusement, when my pastime was obtruded upon by the, of course, unwelcome visit of the ladies! However, they proved this time good company. And as I had long since learned to like my step-mother very much, I did feel, on the whole, rather glad to have a little company-talk with Mother and Co. We immediately launched into the performance of a sea-side drama, which resulted in welding another link to my chain of events.

The actors were step-mother, grown sister, Gentile lady, and this little self.

Sister. "You are enjoying yourself finely—got any shells?"

"Don't you feel lonesome? come walk with us!" begged mother.

Gentile. "Jonas, how did you like your dinner to-day?"

"Very well," I said, rather unconcernedly, however.

Gentile. "Wasn't that meat excellent? you ate heartily, I noticed."

Self. "I tell *you!* but it was good, and I was *so* hungry."

She smiled knowingly, while *my* ladies tried in vain to look sober.

Such conduct naturally excited in me a suspicion that all was not right; but what was wrong, I knew not. I knew very well that I was not poisoned. What could be the matter? In a moment it occurred to me that perhaps I had eaten PORK. I was frightened! "Did *you* go to the market for it?" I imploringly asked. "Yes," she replied. "Was it *pork?*" She looked at the company out of the corner of her eye: they chuckled; she forced a smile, and slowly answered, "Y-e-e-s."

My mind for a moment staggered. I cast a reproving glance at the deceivers, and yelled out, "You hyp-pr-pr-pr." The stammering elongation of the word was occasioned by a sudden grasp of my older sister, who shook me so hard that before I could get "it" out, it was out, that is the pork came to an untimely exit, giving a peculiar emphasis to my unfinished "hypocr-ite." "For G—'s sake," they profanely begged, "don't tell anybody when we get back to London."

The secret was all *out* now, and my feelings may be more easily imagined than described. I looked imploringly into their faces. There was no help for me. Father also was silent, as the pork went on digesting. O! what a dilemma! I had committed a great sin, and was truly penitent. But I could not find a soul to sympathize with me. Had I been in London I should have gone at once to the Chief Rabbi and confessed. But I was nearly eighty miles from him. A thousand thoughts flashed like phantoms through my terrified mind, and it would not have required much argument to make me believe that I heard the *actual hog grunt*.

Maddened at the consummate hypocrisy of my relatives, I determined—if possible—to swallow an emetic. I ran out of the house (to which we had returned) to find a druggist, so that I might put my purpose into execution. But before I reached one, my better judgment resumed the ascendency. I concluded that my sin would rest upon those by whom I had been deceived. As for me, I would live and die, a Jew. Then I should be saved in spite of hogs, Christians, and hypocrites.

So far I have given the reader a faint idea of the miry clay in which the poor Jew is plunged. How well adapted to their leaders is the reproof of the ever-considerate Saviour: "Ye blind guides! ye strain at a gnat, and swallow a camel."

Looking at the past from my present position, I am sometimes led to wonder why I did not in those days take a more sensible view of my own standing. Neither myself nor any other Jew had the least scruple concerning acts of immorality, under whatever circumstances committed. Following implicitly in the footsteps of my predecessors, I lied, cheated, and swore with impunity, never feeling conscious of having done wrong until my quiet was disturbed by having forsooth eaten in ignorance a piece of pork! Amidst all this confusion, I was in the habit of saying a prayer for everything I could hear, see, taste, touch, or smell; even for thunder, lightning, and every imaginable thing. Jesus fitly says " all their works they do to be seen of men." O, Christians, when you read your New Testament, hear preached the Gospel of Jesus Christ; when you stretch forth your hands and humble your souls before the one throne of Jehovah, then do think of, pity and pray for fallen Israel, as you yearn over the utterly blind. Remember too, that if the Eternal God, for the accomplishment of his own gracious purposes, keeps the Jew a distinct *man;* it is the very Judaism of to-day that keeps him distinct and incorrigibly as through and through a sinner, the more so if not hopelessly so, because seemingly religious.

CHAPTER VII.

AN ALTERED PROGRAMME.

I cannot now remember how long my season of recreation lasted, but it matters not to either you or me. When the time arrived for me to return to school, I was informed that the establishment had removed to a beautiful section of country named Hammersmith; so thither I repaired to resume my studies. Upon arriving I found that we had reason to be pleased with the change of location.

There were other changes also for the better, which gave us entire satisfaction. The first was the resignation by Rabbi Mosha Eleazer Solomon, of his position, which had passed temporarily into the hands of his two sons, Shemuile and Zalmer. I must say that we liked both of them; they were more thoroughly modernized in every respect. It had long been painfully evident (as our backs often testified, and our stomachs bore witness) that a reform was needed.

Some of the improvements were of a high order. It was necessary to fill the vacancy made by the rabbi's resignation. This was done by the acquisition of a superior model of a man, who, though a Gentile, was a finished gentleman, and an eminent scholar. He and Zalmer took the English and scientific departments. Then we had a large burly Frenchman, Monsieur Shobert, as professor of modern languages. He took snuff out of a shovel, one shovelful to each nostril. There remained Shemuile, assisted occasionally by Zalmer, as professor of Hebrew literature. These things, with much more, gave us all a new zest for our school. There were reforms in the regimen also, which we had reason to exult over. And first, we were not, as heretofore, *allowanced* in our rations. Secondly, we were assured that the bread should never again be mouldy. Thirdly, fresh meat was to be provided twice a week instead of once, as hitherto. Fourthly, we were to have a little mustard. The doctor said mustard was a good vermifuge. It was, therefore, desired as preventing a profitless consumption of food.

After Shemuile had enlightened us upon these and kindred delightful topics, and had fairly arrived at the end, one of the boys (I dare not tell his name) here put a question, greatly to the merriment of all the old Brixton pupils. "Are you going to make us drink Epsom salts?" he asked. Down went the rattan on the desk. Silence! We obeyed. But let me indicate why hatred fell on salts. When a boy, I did so dislike to drink a solution of these. Now our Spring vacation occurred in April, in time for the Passover festival. Toward the close of the term, old Mosha used to make us march in single file to the breakfast table. At the door stood a waiter to hand each boy a tin-cup full of salts; and Mosha himself was sentinel, to see that every boy swallowed every drop, *inside* his neck, before he

could enter.   The other teachers were stationed
along the rear, to prevent skulking.   Mosha used to
tell us that it was good for us to drink salts before
Passover; it helped to "purge out the old leaven."
As a running commentary on his words, was to be
noticed the very rapid running out of the school-
room during that eventful day.   This originated
many a hard speech, the hardest imprecating saline
medicaments.

School days were now gliding along pleasantly
enough under the new order of things.   No more
hungry mouths, and (considering our deserts) comparatively few smarting backs.   Our gentlemanly
Gentile teacher, Mr. P., (O how we all loved him!)
exerted a finer moral influence over us than we ever
dreamed of.   In fact there was a perceptible improve-
ment in our two Hebrew teachers also.   They proved
to us now that they too were gentlemen, and capable also of exerting a moral influence.   Heretofore,
I had received several applications of rattan as an
effectual remedy for carelessness.   Its more careful
use now made me more careful.   For Shemuile was
a good metaphysician, and observing that such rem-
edies aggravated the moral disease, one day returned
my arithmetical entry-book without even a scolding.
I received the book with a very broad grin (and my
mouth was not the smallest;) then nudging my right-
elbow chum, I wrote upon my slate, good for me!
Upon opening the book a short time afterward, I
discovered that Shemuile had written something on
the bottom of the page.   It was handsomely executed in blue ink.   I read it.   My face insensibly

elongated. Somebody said to me just then, "what's the matter, Jonie?" I pointed to the "hand-writing." "Assiduous at study yet negligent in entering his various sums." My pride was roused. Shemuile had cured me.

Satisfied as I felt with my school, nothing was sufficient to erase from my mind the impressions which the Margate deception had made. I felt that, should anything more transpire akin to it, it would be attended with very serious results. As it had already happened, its tendency varied. Sometimes I hated Christians more for it, then I blamed Mrs. B. exclusively. But in the main it only served to expose the fallacy of Judaism. I never spoke of the circumstance to any one; but my mind would not lie at rest, my conscience was only lulled by the reflection that I was still secure in "Abraham."

As time thus passed along and I enjoyed the rule of my new masters, a circumstance occurred which seriously disturbed my equanimity. One day while the Hebrew class was chanting the lesson, we were visited by Rabbi Mosha. As a rule it devolved upon me principally to chant a special portion assigned to a particular occasion. This season happened on the Sabbath following the next fourth day of April, at which time I should be thirteen years old. But I will speak of that event in its turn.

Rabbi Mosha was certainly unusually prolific in yarns of "the same old sort." And somebody's skepticism kept pace with him. At length recess was announced. Shut within a high brick wall enclosure, six months at a time, it was difficult for lively boys to live, forever playing with the self-same ball. We wanted some new plaything. Rabbi Mosha had given us an idea. "Boys, let's play 'Christians,'" sounded a voice. This proposition brought the crowd to a stand-still. "How shall we do it?" was the echo. On it went, "I know, I'll tell yur, I'll show yur." "Who's got a piece of chalk?" "That's the thing." A large cross was now made on the wall. This done, we all tumbled down on our knees before it, and every sinner of us made as queer a noise and as ugly a grimace as possible. While we were in this posture, exercising ourselves in very strange gesticulations, with minds absorbed in our tragi-comedy, "witch of Endor," and representation of kindred spirits,—Rabbi Zalmer detected us! In a moment he flew into high passion. Equally as quick we were upon our feet. Some of us had our faces chalked; others had laughed until tears came, leaving their faces begrimed with dirt; some were angry because the sport was spoiled, and others again trembled for the consequences. There we stood, an amateur band of auto-de-fe, before poor Zalmer. He marched us one by one into the school-room. Order first, "Lay down your caps." This is done. Order second, "Take off your coats and vests." These left us. Then he commenced at the head of the column, and with a stiff rattan inflicted a most unmerciful flagellation upon every one of us in turn. Some yelling arose then, but when *afterwards* we received our lecture that we ought not to imitate the Christians even in jest, some of our teeth set firmly, and a spirit said "You lie." At length we were set at liberty, vowing vengeance upon the instrument of our torture, which we split before night. Mr. P., the Gentile teacher, looked on meanwhile from his silent rostrum, pale as death.

Murmuring and mutiny were the further results of this whole transaction. We actually envied our sisters at home who were free from such penance. We soon found a chance to exhibit our bruised backs to each other. "Would I were a girl," I said, "they don't have to go through such everlasting 'Rosha and Gemara' stuff o' nonsense." Here one of the boys reminded me of a "prayer" we should all have to say every morning of our lives after we are thirteen years old. "I thank thee, Father, King of the universe, that thou hast not made me a woman." For the time being I forgot my punishment and laughed right out. "I've only seen one time," said I, "that I uttered that prayer. Last summer when I was at home, my sisters were going to a ball. While they were dressing, my younger sister set to bawling for me to come and hook her dress, as all the other hands were engaged. I set to work, getting my knee against her back and pulling lustily. The hooks slipped in their eyes with a click. I got the last in, and there stood my charming sister looking more like a wasp than a girl. Selin, I now asked, are you going to dance skewered up in this way? She put her hands on her sides and—belched! 'Thank God I'm not a woman,' I added." This narration brought out a general laugh, and restored order and obedience.

But with me the tragedy did not end here. I

could not become reconciled to the bigotry that had imposed upon me so severe a flogging. Several days afterwards, I was careless about my prayers and everything of a Jewish character. I could not for my life understand how religion of any kind could be crammed into a boy's head (I never thought about the heart) by torturing his back. Thus I reasoned and murmured, until the very sight of an adult Jew filled me with disgust. After many days, however, I became more reconciled, and in a magnanimous, forgiving spirit, I exclaimed, " O Judah, with all thy faults I love thee still."

There is certainly a meaning in the proverb, " Experience is the wisdom of fools." In my case it was eminently verified. Thus it came to pass that a combination of circumstances, some trifling and others weighty, had a tendency to point out to me the defects of Judaism, and ultimately to lead me to my Saviour.

Every new development made me more sensitive to the defects of my religion. But being religiously inclined, I was constrained to adhere to the only apparently fair claim of Judaism; that is, to arrogate Heaven to myself by virtue of my blood relation to Abraham. Thus I continued to walk in the footsteps of my forefathers. Abraham went before: Moses followed after; and we Jews will certainly follow on—this was my constant boast. But it is now many years since the Lord dispelled that awful illusion. I have found Him who is before Abraham —a true Moses. In *my* dear Jesus my soul delights.

On Him alone I hang for salvation. Dear reader, do you know and love Him too?

"Know ye my Saviour, know ye my Saviour,
Know ye my Saviour and God?
O! He died on Calvary,
To atone for you and me,
And to purchase salvation with blood."

Nothing is more common than for a man to plead conscience and sincerity, as he "steals the livery of Heaven to serve the devil in." This was true of Saul of Tarsus, who thought he was doing service to God when butchering the Christians. It is also true of every Jew in the world, who vainly believes that he is serving God by rejecting the glorious "Mediator between God and man." Thus it was that my conscience always either "accused or excused" me. It "accused" me for adhering to a religion which I *knew* to be defective. It "excused" me upon the ground of ignorance of a remedy. And although I had a disposition to serve God, my confidence in the "Priesthood" was still so great that I concluded, whatever my sins, they would provide means to "pay every debt and cancel every obligation" to the Almighty for my salvation.

Many an honest observer has remarked the great similarity between the ceremonies of the Jewish and Roman churches, and been led to exclaim, "why this is just like the Catholic's ritual!" while in fact the Roman is but a poor caricature of the Jewish, and modern Judaism is a corruption of the Mosaic system. Still it holds the mind in abject bondage.

How swiftly the arrow of time flies when suffered

5

to steer its course without resistance.   But how
tardily it drags along to the mind which is appren-
ticed to be for years, daily burdened with a ponder-
ous weight of unmeaning indigestible religious forms,
from which, in darkness, it struggles to be free.
This was too true of myself.   An afflicted burden at
home, I was left to be educated by bigoted Jews
abroad.   Thus rolled on my precious time, while
the prejudice of education every day contributed to
engulph me deeper in the abyss of a religionism
from which my inquiring mind could obtain no
satisfactory answer.   Now I know that the "eye of
the Lord" was upon me all the time, and in His own
manner in due time, He brought to light means for
my deliverance.   "Bless the Lord, O my soul, and
all that is within me, bless His holy name."

CHAPTER VIII.

Dear reader, are you anxious to read any more of my history? Presuming that you may be, I will open this division, as recording what transpired on the fourth day of April, in the year of our Lord, one thousand eight hundred and twenty-five, at which ever-memorable epoch I arrived at the vastly important age of thirteen years. A new era opens for the Jewish lad at this time of life. Mysteries that shrouded his former days now resolve themselves into a huge enigma. I will, therefore, first simply "state the question," and secondly, I will elucidate by an example, most mathematically.

First. He is now "of age." Twelve years used to be the period, but the rabbins, being very honest, allow a "baker's dozen."

Second. He is rabbinically capable of taking care of himself.

Third. Anciently he might disinherit himself by receiving from his father his "portion of goods," at this time. This practice, though *supposed* to have been customary in the East, is rarely repeated by European Jews. It may throw some light upon the parable of the "Prodigal Son," as recorded by the Evanglist, Luke xv: 11 to the end.

67

Fourth. He then receives his phylacteries. Hold on, reader, don't be impatient. I promised to elucidate.

Fifth. He is taken into the number necessary to the ten, for saying certain important prayers.

Sixth. He must chant a portion of the Law in the synagogue on the Sabbath succeeding his birth-day.

Seventh. He goes home and feasts like an epicure.

Among every class of people, times and seasons are differently observed, agreeably to the laws of the religion they profess. The thirteenth year of a Jewish boy's life is the second time that brings him into special notice. The first is at his circumcision, on the eighth day of his age, at which time he receives his name. The second is the period we are now considering. The little chap anticipates that day with considerable emotion. I well remember what peculiar hallucination enchanted my visionary brain when that day was approaching. Castles of gigantic proportion, and unheard-of splendor, were fancifully and rapidly originated. Then I should be a *man*. Then I should be introduced to the congregation in "Shule"—synagogue. Then I should wear "Tefelen"—phylacteries, as other men. And above all, father said that I should have a new suit of "sky blue." O hasten the *holy* day for the sake of the—sky blue! Please remember that I am all this time in school, and ad interim, aye for several weeks previous, I have been kept a close student and rehearser in chanting the portion that would fall to my lot in regular order. I labored hard to acquire the correct pronunciation, accent and tone of every word. I had too much pride to make a failure. But so little did I care either for the translation of my portion into English or any other language, or for the sanctity of the occasion, that one week afterwards I had entirely forgotten which had been my portion. After much hard labor, I successfully surmounted every obstacle, and before the time arrived I was in readiness for the—sky blue.

This O-be-joyful day necessarily called me home a few days before the Passover vacation; so bidding a good-bye to many choice companions, and receiving a warm pressure of the Gentile, Mr. P.'s, hand, in due time I arrived at home.

All the previous night (O how long it was!) I held myself in readiness to—"prevent the dawning of the morning?" No, but to *anticipate* it. By eight o'clock A. M., our regular breakfast time, I was ready to be seen. My toilet was completed, hair perfumed, (curling naturally as it did all over my head,) shirt collar stiff to the cutting of my ears, shoes too tight for my corns; and O how heavenly a prospect of perfect sky blue! The suit was bought of Mr. Moses Cohen, and was sacredly Jewish. It consisted of pants, (of course,) vest, and a tight round-about. Now, one more pull at the buckle of my cravat, which was already choking me till my pale face turned red, and I made my august appearance at the breakfast table.

"Sholum Alichem," greeted me from all present. I have endeavored in this reproduction to anglicise two Hebrew words. I am obliged to make use of these and a few others, but I will show the reader how to pronounce them understandingly. In the first word you give (agreeably to Polish usage) a long sound to the " o " and you have the word. The second has for its " a " the sound given in " far ; " its " li " sounds naturally; its " ch " is as in " chem," when the mouth is shaped as if for a laugh, and an effort made at clearing the throat, but with an out-breathing slightly terminating in " m." Now you can talk Hebrew: what an acquisition! The words are a beautiful salutation. They mean, " Peace (prosperity) be unto you !" You find a similar salutation and reply given by Boaz, in Ruth ii: 4. You may refer to it with advantage, as to all other references that may be indicated.

I was taught to receive this beautiful and earnest salutation by reversing the words for a reply. So when the family said " Sholum Alichem," I replied " Alichem Sholum," or " To yourselves" rather would I summon this " welfare." Trembling as I was with fear for the coming Sabbath, struggling no less with pride of heart, and squirming under the pressure of choking cravat and tight shoes, the adaptation of my answer to the kind salutation, evoking it, is best set forth in the case of an Indian who could talk but little English, and was pursuing a Frenchman, (to make matters worse,) for Monsieur's coveted scalp. The red man ran toward him with raised tomahawk. " Me want scalp." At this the Frenchman swore and started off. The race is swift and exciting. Indian gains ground; Frenchman roars and runs on. Indian, however, soon gets near enough to give one mighty bound. With his

left hand he has now caught the hatless Frenchman
by the hair of his head.   His right arm raised on
high, brandishes his tomahawk.   But, away runs
the Frenchman, his wig only in the Indian's hand.
"Over the hills and far away" speeds Monsieur,
leaving the surprised and chagrined Indian transfixed
in attitude, gazing first at the wig, then at the tomahawk, then, O so longingly, at the Frenchman, far,
far away.   Finding that his prey was literally gone,
he gloomily looked once more at the wig, exclaiming,
but not in French, "dats von pig lie."—Not in
words, however, did I echo this view of affairs; and
nothing of the kind being suspected, my sky blue
underwent another general examination.   Everybody said I looked very fine.   I felt all too "fine."
Everybody was satisfied; as was I also—after breakfast.

How my heart beats!   "Shobbos," Sabbath, has
come.   I am actually in the great synagogue.   No
wonder I'm trembling with nervous excitement.   At
the proper time, or when the chanter has arrived at
my portion, father and I are "called up."   Here I
must explain a little to my unenlightened reader.
The "Law of Moses" is divided into fifty-four portions, one of which must be chanted on every Sabbath.   Now also the Pentateuch, or the first five
books of the Old Testament, must be carried with
ceremony from its ark to the reader's desk at the
centre of the house.   So the clerk puts up at auction
the privilege of doing this, the highest bidder—fair
play now!—gets it.   During the chanting exercise,
several persons are "called up" to the desk, whose

business it is to gather up the four corner fringes of
his "tallith," (which I will explain by-and-by,) and
touch them on the next division or small portion to
be chanted, and then remain to hear it recited. For
this privilege, he makes a small or large payment,
just as he is inclined, then he receives a blessing and
—pays for it, then he orders blessings for other parties, sometimes for many, sometimes for few; but
always he is to pay for each and all. He has no
sooner finished than another member, called up, in
like manner buys himself rich. In this way every
man, who has money, to be sure is through the year
favored by being "called up." Finally the Pentateuch is again carried home, by auction of course,
and rests until it is wanted for a like purpose once
more.

Here stood father and I right at our post. A
certain stiffness took hold on the spine of my back,
as I walked along in my "sky blue" by the side of
my father up to the very rostrum. Once "in for it,"
I summoned up all my courage and at once determined to "fight it out on this line if it took a long
summer" of burning embarrassment. And I did
it too. I went through the performance most manfully. Father felt proud of such a boy. What
father would not have been thus exercised? He
paid for piles of blessings that day. I do not know,
in fact I never learned how many I got; but at the
time there was one thing I very well knew, it was
that I would have preferred the *price* of them. Our
ladies were up in the gallery, the place assigned for
them; for no where else in the sanctuary dare their

feet tread. Remember, "I thank Thee, Father, King of the universe, that Thou hast not made me a—woman."

But on being dismissed, we all met at the outside entrance and walked home together. Thus passed the " great day." At its close quiet is restored to my very nervous system, and I am left to find out the meaning and utility of all this ceremony any way I—cannot. I had carried my " sky blue" through the entire Passover festival. Having a sense of my consequence as a little above a "sky blue round-about;" I had given it a rather rougher usage than such material is used to, and the miserable thing, some how or other, split open in the back clear up to the collar. So I must have a new one. I begged for one of another color. But the ladies said that it would not match. I submitted!

A few days remained before I was to return to school. I will endeavor to fill up this interval profitably and fulfil my promise to give the reader a little description of the phylacteries.

Everybody around reminds me that I'm " B'mitz-vo." What's *B'mitzvo?* you ask. I reply, anything, providing it has no force to its meaning. Call it " thirteen," or " of age;" either will do. For my part, I was so troublesome in making inquiries of everybody who seemed likely to know, that at last some one informed me that *now* my father ceases to be longer responsible for my sins. Who then is? asked I. " Why yourself." What makes me responsible? I persisted. " Why, you are ' B'mitzvo.'" What must I do? " You must be a good Yehudah

(Jew.") What must I do to be a good Yehudah? "Say your prayers, wear your Tefelen, go to Shule, keep the Law, obey the rabbins; then living and dying a Yehudah, it will be all right with you at last. Now do you, reader, know what "B'mitzvo" really means? I aver that I do not!

Imagine, as the practical result, that you see me next morning, standing in the parlor facing the East. Prayer-book is in hand, and I am adorned with my phylacteries. Father and brother Abraham also were there in similar costume. I felt consequentially devout. I would not miss a single letter. Father got through first and left the room. I noticed that just then my brother began to take off his "Tefelen." I took the hint and stopped off short. Turning to my brother, "Abe," whispered I, "what's these things for?" The fact that he gave me this horrible answer, is my apology for repeating his words. "D—d if I know," and off he went. And so did I —it might have been as if shot. I confess that I was led to indulge some ludicrous reflections relative to the peculiar utility of these unmeaning things with which I had to be encumbered every day of life. No explanation had been given me. Enough for me to know that I *must* wear them. I well re-member once having on my foreign livery and being impelled to look into the mirror. The effect was so ridiculous that I laughed right out. I thought I looked like a clown with a fool's cap on. But for the sake of peace, I concluded to yield, adopting, however, my brother's provoked yet fearful rejoinder.

By this time you may find me back at my old

school quarters again.   I really felt glad to meet once
more my former companions in blind bigotry.   Some
of us had grown up together in the same school from
childhood.   But, being "B'mitzvo" now, I was led
to regard as mere youngsters those chums who were
a few months in the minority relatively.   Many a
perplexing congratulation did I receive because I
was B'mitzvo.   I couldn't help that.   But nobody
meant any harm.   The jokes of the boys at least
were more innocent than the Sholum alichem of
the rabbins.   So I bore everything in good humor,
save once.   A *youngster* had improvised a couplet
badly rhymed or tortured in orthography.   It was
in allusion to that delicate matter, the appearance of
my virgin "goose down."

> "Had a good time B'mitzvo Jonie?
> Why didn't yu stay till yr beard be growne?"

I did not reply to this fraternal pleasantry, and
thus in a few days I was permitted to study on as
hard as ever and quite as unmolested.   In lapse of
time and "by hook or by crook," I gathered a little
light upon my phylacteries, but I never learned the
full truth about them until in after years when I
read Christian books.

Now, dear reader, I want you to promise me that
you will open your Bible and read where I refer
you.   A record of the origin of phylacteries is unknown to anybody.   The Talmudical Jews found
their authority on two portions of scripture.   These
are, Numbers xv: 37 to the end, and Deut. vi: 8–9.
Now, nothing can be plainer to an unbiased mind
than that the All-wise designed by these outward

vestments to bring constantly before the minds of his people their great duty to obey all the precepts of the law. The priest's peculiar uniform, as well as much more of similar character, was adapted to the condition of affairs at the time of their institution. In that day there was a degree of intelligence which regulated Israel's worship. But now, meagre as the provision may appear to the Christian, yet it is true that the Jews look upon their phylacteries as a kind of charm to keep off infernal spirits.

Upwards of five hundred years, a colony of Jews have been settled in the Crimea. They are called Karaites by the Talmudists, on account of their rejection of the claims of the Talmud over their consciences, and their intelligent adherence to the grammatical construction of a text in preference to any rabbinically garbled mystery. They do not wear Tefelen, and say that the Talmudists, in wearing them, are "bridled asses." But, brother Karaite, be gentle. I'm not responsible for the accident of birth; yet many a time while wearing them I have agreed with you.

I propose now to give the reader a brief description of these "spirit drivers." The number of them is *five*, some say but four. The first is called M'zuzah. This is a hollow tube nailed on the right side post of every room in the house. Two "portions" are enclosed, namely, Deut. vi: 4-10, and xi: 13-21. These are soldered in forever; the word "Shaddai" alone is to be seen through an opening cut in the tin. As I must be very brief, I can only say that *every* thing connected with it must be approved by the rabbis, even to the two small nails that hold it. Now when a Jew leaves a room, (some say passes either way,) he must touch " Shaddai," and then kiss the favored fingers. He must *never* remove it, under penalty of " sudden death to his children," unless a Gentile is to occupy as the next tenant; in that case he *must* remove the—what do you call it ?

The second is a part of the *bridle*, called " Tsitsith;" the Hebrew letters of which word have an aggregate numerical value of six hundred. This is made of any old piece of fabric. You take simply two four-cornered pieces about six inches long either way, and unite them by means of straps long enough to rest upon either shoulder, so as to allow the squares to rest one against the breast and the other opposite, between the shoulders. At the four corners are fastened fringes, each having eight threads knotted in rotation five times; so that, $8+5+600=613$, you have the number of precepts the rabbins say are in the Law.

When a boy, I used sometimes to say to my grandma, " What are these things for on the doors, grandma?" " The ' Torahs Mosha' say they must be, my dear." This satisfied me then. But when I became " B'mitzvo "—a man, thirteen years old, I felt quite competent to demand of wiser heads, " What is the meaning of the ' tsitsith?' " " Torahs Mosha, Laws of Moses, require it." To which was added a monotone admonition to the effect that " every good ' Yehudah' wears it all day long under his clothes; when, therefore, he goes abroad, *no harm can come to him.*" Of course I did not argue the point, but concluded rather to watch for the effects; and I always found that the virtue of "tsitsith" is fully as prodigious as that of the second part, a horse-shoe nailed—not on the hoof—but on your premises, and for precisely the same purpose. But then, I was as ignorant of that wonderful arithmetical mystery, $8+5+600=613$ precepts, as I was of the inside of the M'zuzah, or first-named phylactery. But RABBI says so!

O give me that which my mind digests, that warms my heart, and makes me a better man. I have it now before me, and my heart swells with gratitude, my eyes grow blind with tears of worship, as I read and apply to my heart and life daily—not six hundred and thirteen—but, "*two* commandments" on which "hang all the law and the prophets." Blessed reduction now graciously possible of fulfillment.

The third part is called "Tallith," or "Great tallith." It is a large cloth, sufficient to cover the whole upper part of the body. The fringes at the corners are of the same sort as those mentioned above. The rabbins say that it must be made of white lamb's wool. This is formally kissed on the upper centre piece (which is generally ornamented,) and then thrown over the head at the time of prayer, but suffered to slip down and rest on the shoulders in warm weather. It has five broad stripes along the lower edge, to remind you that there are five books of Moses, the "Torahs Mosha." Every operation in its manufacture must be performed by Jewish hands. The wool is to be entirely shorn, not a single particle being pulled off the animal.

The animal itself must be approved by a rabbi, and slaughtered ceremoniously by a Jew. Only one thing (a sad deficiency) mars all this—but Judaism is excusable for that, because the rabbins could not remedy the sore evil—the lamb could not bleat *in Hebrew*. Alas! poor Ba-ah, thy bleating well terminates in an ah!

The remaining two parts of the "bridle" are so much alike, that I will, for brevity's sake, speak of them together. The first is called "Rosch," head, the other "Yadh," designating the arm and "hand." They are small, square boxes, made of parchment or vellum, which have deposited in them detached portions of the Law, and are firmly closed. Fine calfskin loops are attached, one for the head to go through, and there are also two long thongs which hang down in front on either side, while the box itself rests directly on the forehead between the eyes. The other loop is for the left arm, which is bared. The loop being drawn tight enough to suffer the second box to rest on front of the arm above the elbow, the thong is then wrapped around the arm ten times, being thus brought to the tenth letter of the alphabet, "Yod"—a sacred letter when doubled. The remainder of the thong is laid about the hand in the shape of the letter "Shin." The same letter is stamped on the sides of the boxes. It is the first letter of "Shaddai," Almighty, found on the "M'zuzah."

The Jew attaches an undue importance to these silly things. Even now may be seen, as I have actually surveyed, scores of the boxes, made quite large and then worn enclosed in a thin brass case. The bulky dimensions of the phylacteries render their use ridiculous in the extreme, and it is a great marvel that so many very intelligent men, to be met in the Jewish ranks, continue blindly to insult the ever blessed Jehovah with such nonsensical stuff. And our discerning Jesus administered a fair reproof when he said, "All their works they do, to be seen of men: they make broad their phylacteries, and enlarge the borders of their garment." Matthew xxiii: 25.

This is the meaning of the word itself, as Webster gives it; "in a *general sense* any charm, spell, or amulet, worn as a preservative from danger or disease," is a phylactery.

But while it is true that not one Jewish boy in five hundred either knows or cares what good there is *inside* of these, or of what advantage they are as put on the *outside* of his body, all and each wear them daily, not daring to neglect them through fear that "something might turn up."

Thus it was with myself all the time I wore them, and when in after years I began to neglect them, I acted like a would-be Christian whiskey-tipler, sneaking from the eye of man to indulge his sinful (!) propensity.

But now I am the Lord's free man. Thirty-four years ago, I laid aside both phylacteries and alcohol. Since then I have found no use for either: they are both alike delusive and treacherous. In Jesus Christ I have not received the spirit of bondage again to fear, but I have received the spirit of adoption,

whereby I cry, Abba, (that is, Father.) O, my
Heavenly Father, see my tears, hear my prayer,
save, O save the Jews!

6

CHAPTER IX.

PROGRESS, ALIAS RETROGRESSION.

Since I last informed you, dear reader, that I had returned to my school, one entire year of school-time has again rolled around. I have been home once, and now, at my fourteenth year, I am to spend my birth-day at home, bidding a final and not reluctant adieu to boarding-school. The Passover festival being ended, the question of a disposition of me for the future was very seriously considered by my dear father. I confess that I demurred at the idea of returning to a Jewish school, and my reasons were mostly buried in the mental reservation I preserved. I pleaded, however, that I had enough Hebrew to carry me to Heaven, and I wanted to advance in my English studies. In consequence of my affliction, father was grievously at a loss to know what he had best do with poor me. It was my own wish to attend for some time yet a high school at home. An indulgent parent was not long deciding to let me have my own way; so climbing over his con-science, he sent me to a first-class *Gentile* school in London to finish (as he said) my education. This was a great advance in my life.

But here new difficulties started into existence. One was the fact that my prejudices were already

immovably fixed. How could *I* submit to Gentile
rule? Another was my attachment for the " good (?)
old way." There was still another. They used to
read prayers (not the Bible) at opening and closing
of school. This difficulty, however, was overcome
by a forced consent, by late attendance, and early
retirement, so that my deaf ears were not offended
by the name—Christ. To facilitate this arrange-
ment, my desk was isolated. This manœuvre, however, soon rendered me conspicuous; so being the
only Jew in the school, I was subjected to a great
deal of taunt and derision. All petty vexations I
endured peaceably. But when the boys resorted to
the persecuting medium so familiar to the vulgar,
whose little souls cannot bear the idea of allowing a
man to possess his God-given, inalienable right
simply because he is forsooth a Jew—when they
invoked the assistance of the *hog* as their ally, and
flung at me in the open air their pestiferous shouts:

> " I had a piece of pork,
> And I stuck it on a fork,
>   *   *   *   *   * "

Then it was that I began to *realize* that I detested
Christians. Such odious repetitions made me peev-
ish and distant, and turning upon my mock-heroic
comrades a look of unutterable disdain, I retorted
with a deep curse, calling them " Sons of the *hang'd
one.*" Surely I had not forgotten Margate!

I do not remember how long I remained at this
school, but it was not so long as it otherwise would
have been. When I left, it was to try the experiment over again elsewhere with somewhat better

results. In process of time, however, I bid adieu
entirely to schools both Jewish and Gentile. I at
last grew tired of books; so I laid them all aside,
never for a moment dreaming that in less than five
years from that time, I should be commanded by the
Eternal Jehovah—blessed be His name—to take hold
on them again, with scores of others of a loftier character, and study them night and day, that I might
qualify myself to be a *vicar* in a church, holding out
the cross of my ever-adorable, ever-glorious Jesus.

My hatred for Christians, meanwhile, became
greater than ever, although I was by no means blind
to the serious defects of Judaism. Nor was I without lively anxiety, and some inquiry even, as to how
I could mend the matter. In imagination, I applied
many a vain remedy. Sometimes I attributed the
existing imperfections to my want of discernment.
Then I would look about me for one, if but one
faithful follower of Moses; but all in vain. When,
therefore, I could not find a single Mosaic ceremony
observed according to the original pattern, I des-
paired outright. Thus, admitting Moses himself to
be the judge, and looking not beyond his dispensation, every Jew in the world stands condemned!

As the storm-beaten mariner will rush to the
nearest port, so acted I in my perplexity.

> "To Sinai's fiery mount I fled;
> It poured its curses on my head."

But I knew no other refuge! With such a prospect before me, I suffered as if out of time the penalty of an anxious but rayless mind. What was I to
do? From no earthly source could I derive light or

instruction. Finding myself in such a dilemma, I was compelled to be as much as possible at rest in my ignorance. Hemmed in on every side, my only available refuge was to take advantage of my life-long training, and settle down confidently, satisfied in my " blood relation" to Abraham as availing me for salvation.

Enjoying affluence and improved health, with rapidly advancing maturity of years, I was like the fabled viper which, when restored in pity's bosom to warmth and life, turned against its cherishing friend and bit remorselessly his dear children. Thus I misimproved the blessings with which my kind Heavenly Father had surrounded me. I launched into guilty extremes, yielding to the desires of my wicked heart, now most devoutly engaged in the service of sin. I hungered after vice; with greedi-ness I devoured it, solacing myself by the reflection that one no less than Abraham's son will certainly be finally saved. But for me there was no reprover. With propriety I might have confronted the thirty thousand Jews at that time in the city of London, and demanded : If one of your number, whether he be a rabbi or a layman, in his own conscience actu-ally knows himself to be any better than I, let him come forward and give me the very first genuine reproof, or " cast the first stone."

A stringent law which lies on the shelf as a dead letter in the statute book, is an incubus upon society. And if we apply this to Judaism, we only set forth a fact, for here exist general rules, a gigantic code of ethics, containing in detail six hundred and thirteen precepts, every one of which is but feebly enforced, or (more truthfully speaking) is not enforced at all. Nay, when this general statute is actually violated with glaring impunity by the very men who should force obedience, not by precept only, but by their example, and who loudly profess to do so, is it any wonder that I, a giddy boy, should follow in their track, by a less dishonorable because open disregard of all that is truthful, good, and pure? Therefore there followed a consequent recklessness of the claims of practical Judaism. Hence, one by one, my daily round of religious ceremonies was laid aside. "Dust to dust."

A first liberty was taken with my "Tefelen." Those useless and unmeaning baubles! I determined that at least I would not longer be a "*Bridled* ass" for their sake. This violation of the rabbinical bull precipitated an unreasonable and senseless reproof. In time, all the ceremonies of my religion grew more tiresome than ever, and I resolved to invent new pretexts for their entire neglect. In this way, while I was obliged to do as others did, to all outward appearance, the very last vestige of sanctity gradually wore itself out. The cause of this may be the better understood when it is known that, step by step I descended the ladder of iniquity, until I became completely baptized in desire for giddy amusements, so that I could no longer find time to read my prayers. And when at seasons I was obliged to give time, the work of an hour was gone over in ten minutes. True, I trembled for the consequences.— Though I had no fear of God, yet I dreaded my father's hasty temper. My fears were shortly realized, for as soon as father found out that I neglected prayers, and particularly Tefelen, he flew into a hurricane of rage at me, and with many a terrible oath, gave vent to his ungovernable passion. Down on my confused pate he poured freely a father's curse; but he did not dream that he was cursing whom Jehovah blessed.

A little reasoning and an intelligent reproof would doubtless have had a salutary effect upon me. But the startling manner in which I was disposed of, originated in my mind the gravest doubts as to my father's sincerity. I learned in fact to swear as hard as he was accustomed to do. This circumstance, connected with many others, had a strong tendency to mollify my favorable prejudices; so much so that I gradually grew more unscrupulous than ever.

The Autumn was approaching, only to increase my dread. Hitherto I had strictly kept all the fasts of the year, especially the one now approaching, called "Yom Kepur," or "Kopher," (covering,) so-called because on that day the sins of the past year are to be "covered." The Law appointed but one fast to be observed. It occurred on the tenth day of the seventh month. See Lev. xvi: 29. But from the time of the Prophet Zechariah, or about five hundred and twenty years before Christ, the Jews reckoned in three more. However, I am to speak of this one only. It arrives at the end of September, and sometimes runs into October. Great preparations of both a moral and a commercial character are very rigidly enforced several days (some say,

nine) previous to the great day. All Jews endeavor
to settle out-lying disputes of every possible nature.
Concessions and restitutions are liberally made, and
forgiveness is everywhere extended. This is indeed
a very pure quality of morality, and although yoked
to a religion unworthy of it, in itself challenges the
imitation of every Christian on earth. This also
may account for the commendatory fact so universally conceded by every intelligent magistrate of the
land, that the Jew as a foreigner is everywhere a
peace-making and law-abiding, inexpensive, and
profitable citizen.

On the afternoon of the ninth day, they prepare
for the ordeal by receiving an extra meal, which is
all that dare be taken until the sunset of the morrow
or tenth day. The rabbins forbid so much as a drop
of water! Thus they represent the command, "Ye
shall afflict your *souls.*" However negligent of religious duties one may have been during the past
year, he must be sure at this time to be on hand.
The synagogues in the whole world, therefore, are
crowded to suffocation. This circumstance, in connection with the numerous extra illuminations, render the atmosphere very offensive.

Many of the men remain with the rabbins all
night in the synagogue; the wiser part, however, go
to their beds. The whole twenty-four hours are
strictly given to religion. During the day, the prayers of the whole year, besides the extra ones for the
occasion, are read. Chanting the Law, singing mel-
odies, making large contributions for benevolent
objects, (always remembering the poor Jews of Ju-

dea) fervent prayer, especially for Jerusalem (while not one in a thousand ever thinks about its topography) and the usual auction mart for sacred privileges, with other unmeaning ceremonies, in number unmentionable, constitute the *sin-pardoning* services of the great "day of Atonement." At sunset the "Raaf," or Chief Rabbi, blows through a horn instrument the peculiar sound called, I think, "Tekeah," as a signal or permission to go home and—do as you have ever done, till the next cover-all rolls around.

As the day approached, I found my mind growing more distracted every hour. Shall I keep this fast? I always had instinctively dreaded the dreadful day. But now I was intelligently looking about me to find where the good results were to be seen. I found none, none! While I am yet deliberating, with mind almost unsettled, lo, the very day is at hand. Conscience demanded that I should decide quickly. I complied. It was with an emphatic NO. That no settled matters—but not without management.

It was a terrible conclusion; and secrecy must be observed, yes, for the sake of my trembling bones. I could not carry out my arrangements, however, except by confiding in our two Gentile servants. They laughed merely and at once promised to help me. For their own sakes I felt they would keep my life-cause secure.

On the first evening in the synagogue, I did well enough. Father resolved to remain all night. The rest of us went home, after brother and I had received strict orders to be in our places early next morning. I advanced the universal good sentiment, "I wish you well over your fast," bidding good night, and now "to-bed-we-go." How I laughed between the sheets at my well-matured, hypocritical plans! But I slept soundly as a tired boy, and did not (strange to note) even dream of a hungry stomach. The morning came on time. I arose very early, and *secured a good breakfast,* so that by the time the family were all dressed, I was peculiarly ready, and we all went to the synagogue together. I did not pray for an emetic this time. Oh, no! My breakfast clung to its quarters as stubbornly as the Margate pork had failed to do.

My younger sister soon complained. Poor girl, she needed her breakfast. She was really too delicate for such a starvation pennance. Still, "hold on, Selin, this is 'Yom Kopher.'" In hole-y silence, we walked to the synagogue, which we all reached, feeling so sick—of course I had to feign being sick too, very sick.

The ladies dragged themselves upstairs to their gallery prison, while I walked erect among crowds of—other men—to my seat. There was my dear father, with phylacteries nobly on, looking awfully woe-be-gone; tired, sick, faint, and sleepy. "Sholum Alichem," said I. But it awoke no reply. A look full of language, a shake of the head, and a pinch of snuff, was the significant answer.

About ten o'clock the ladies went home. Poor slaves, but not of appetite—not yet. No, for they were *so* hungry. Still, they *dare* not eat. At noon, I proposed to my father that I go home *to see how the*

ladies were getting along; to which he assented. But
my real object was to get my dinner, which I
assure you, dear reader, I made sure of before I
returned.

On reaching home, I found all the ladies a-bed.
"Sholum Alichem," shouted I. "Very sick," was
by no means Hebraistically replied. "O you hypocrites," I cried, "this is the way you fast for your
year's sins, is it? In bed all day; sleeping it off, eh?
You hypocrites!" "Very sick, I'm very sick,"
came the apology in concert. Poor creatures, how
much I pitied them. But, as misery likes company,
their sympathies moved them to inquire after father
and everybody else, almost. Of course, they were
sick—*so was I,* apparently. Taking leave of my
impenitent relations, I returned to the synagogue,
feeling fully conscious that I was not playing the
hypocrite against the Almighty, but against a religion, in itself unmeaning, and by the Lord unwar-
ranted, because in it I could not trace the religion
of Moses.

Seated again, I now consoled myself with the
well-*substantiated* belief that I could stand it until
supper time, as well as any of my less favored Ye-
hudahs.

Surveying the synagogue, the scene appeared
doleful. All was confusion. There were in that
one house more than fifteen hundred "persons," or
if we include the women, it would be fair to say two
thousand, all (minus one) starving their bodies for
the fancied good of their souls. Dressed in phylacteries, some taking snuff; others were talking over

business matters; others again were laughing at
their sick neighbors: some swore that they were a
little hungry, and wished for the night. Their critic
played in a sense the hypocrite. Pressing on to
father's side I felt really sad at seeing how distressed
he appeared, which he perceiving, returned a corresponding sympathetic glance, supposing—how truly
—that I was as sick as everybody else. For I *was*
sick, but sick of farces.

In due time the welcome sound of the cornet was
heard. At once the fast ended. The sound had
scarcely died away, when the whole legion rushed
in confusion to the door. It was exactly like rushing off from a steamer, after a sea-sick voyage.

At home, soon reached, we found everything most
bountiful, and quite ready for our reception. Those
wicked, Gentile daughters of the "hanged one" had
certainly done a very handsome thing for *us*, they
had been doing all day for me. The lights were
brilliant, and the supper in every respect grand
enough, shall I say, for the royal family.

In a few minutes all hands were hard at it, making up evidently for lost time. Somehow I ate
comparatively little; in perfect silence too. I was
certainly an object for general pity. The impression
was, that I had suffered so much during the day that
I was actually too sick to eat. *My* sins were pardoned: that was now beyond question. After supper all retired to bed, glad unmistakably that the
day of voluntary famine was at length ended, and
congratulating each other that "Yom Kopher"
comes but once a year.

I do not propose to apologize for what I have written. Yet I am aware that I give offence to my ewish brother who may read this book. He will be offended upon two accounts: first, because I slighted the day, and secondly, because I am bold in speaking about this. But who should be blamed? Let my Jewish brother look at the fact, that every boy is constrained, even compelled to observe it, under penalty.

Then let him also look at the long chain of exercises, both tedious and unmeaning to him. Now, I ask is there one wide-awake boy in a thousand who would not do as I did, if he could? Aye that would he, and very many prove it, and then charge the whole bill to their fathers and rabbis. I am hoping moreover to accomplish two things. One is, to show that the error in my early education led me on step by step, until I fairly awoke to the sophistry and fallacy of the whole system. As a second good, I hope, by the blessing of God, to arouse some of my Jewish brethren to the truth, that they never can make atonement to God for their sins by all the ceremonies of "Yom Kopher," though endlessly repeated—never.

O Israel, you cannot tell why it is that the clouds have not rained upon your heritage for nearly two thousand years. You see that your vineyard is trodden down; the wild boar of the woods has ravaged it; you behold the tents of strangers pitched there; owls mourn there; Satyrs dance there. You see, you know that the frowns of Almighty God gather darkly over it. Yet do you persistantly interpret all in your favor. O Israel, *where* is *your sceptre?* Seek for it, and you will yet find it in the hands of the true " Shiloh," Jesus Christ, the offspring of David, who alone has made atonement on your own Calvary, and that once for all.

CHAPTER X.

If it be weakness to confess that the night after "Yom Kopher" was a decidedly restless one, then I am certainly very weak. My conscience stung me with severe compunctions. As a drowning man thinks of everything in the conscious struggling with death, so I lay upon my bed, reviewing the past and present. All the future was as dark as the past was blank. I tried to think of something tangible, in either my religion or my sin. I would have given mines of gold for one little ray of light. All at once it came to me. Yes, the wished-for ray did come. But alas, it did not come from the right source! it was nothing but rabbinical moon-shine, after all.

I had been taught to turn my face toward the East every day, and once a month to face about and worship the *new moon!* I did it at home when a child. I did it at school in boyhood, and well I remembered how much contumely we used to heap on that farcical idolatry. One evening the announcement was made that the school would stand in a group facing the new moon. I happened not to hear it. Boys passing in a hurry, shouted, "Hurry up, Jonie, the moon will be gone." What's up? I ran too, shouting, what's up? "The new moon, you fool you, don't you see it, up there?" said one, pointing with his finger. "O, ah, y-e-s." Rabbi held a lighted candle and read a prayer to the—new moon. We who were in the rear, however, offered ours extemporaneously. First a push, then a pinch, then a prayer.

> "I see the moon. The moon sees me
> God bless the moon. And God bless me."

This recurrence at once threw me into a fit of laughter, so I fell asleep. I was quite late in rising next morning; I had slept so soundly. During the day I reflected a great deal, and before night concluded that I had not at all wronged God, but only cheated the Jews; so if I could only keep my past day's conduct secret from *them*, I would be safe enough as to results. My origin, at all events, could not be annulled. This placed me upon a footing with the rest of my brethren, who *had* fasted. Thus I also was virtually a white-washed sinner, prepared, like the rest, for another year's experiment.

By some means, however, my roguery leaked out. Still I escaped censure, until after I had embraced Christianity, when with many a bitter oath, my father charged that day's sin upon me, as one of the darkest evidences of my downfall. Experience, the most thorough of schoolmasters, so exposed to me the errors of "Judaism," that ultimately the whole system seemed to be nothing but Judaism in mimicry.

In time, I even doubted if there was such a thing as religion at all; but was ready to yield the palm to Judaism, if there were faith on the earth. If there be but one God, he is assuredly the God of the Jews, reasoned I. Yet here is a religion professing that its origin is Heavenly, though agreeing with its founder in not a single particular, unless we except the bare rite of circumcision. On the contrary, it is full of bigotry and superstition, and withal is maintained by a people professing to be God's peculiar treasure, while swearing with impunity, blaspheming the name of the Lord most appallingly, upon the most trifling occasions too, and anathematizing all other religions that do not wear its peculiar, but unserviceable harness. As a people they fall very far short of what they seem to be—they too, who are the only ones who have any right either to be or seem to be at all. Can there then possibly exist such a thing as religion? Such were my gloomy reflections. I trembled. Still I had a chance for my life. I would hang to a button of Abraham's coat with one hand, and to a single hair of Moses, (not Esau) with the other. So that, after I shall have spent a life in infidelity, I will yet find that Judaism is true, I shall then be able to draw myself near to the law, and on the other hand plead my Abrahamic origin: when, lo, I am saved! Happy expedient; so for the time being, get out of my way, so-called religion!

I remained some time in this state of mind, coasting around, but not daring to launch out into the open sea of infidelity, through fear of something, I knew not what, and meanwhile believing tranquilly that I was sure of salvation in any issue. Yet I feared, I trembled. In me was consciously verified

7

the text, " The wicked flee when no man pursueth."
Thus I continued to trifle with religion from the
borders of infidelity, until at last I fairly marched
forth into open rebellion against the very God of
Heaven.

One day as I walked abroad, my attention was
arrested by a very large poster printed with red ink,
announcing that the " Rev. Robert Taylor" was de-
livering a course of lectures in the Rotunda, on Black
Friar's bridge road, upon the Bible. " There is no
God of either Jews or Christians." Such was the
motto endorsed by the singular placard.

My heart leaped with emotion, as I read the awful
advertisement. Here, blasphemed I, is the truth of
the whole matter: there is no God, no such thing
either as religion : I'll go to hear Robert Taylor, he's
the man for me. A little further on was another
mammoth poster : " Going to raise the devil to-night
at the Rotunda." This looked like trifling, but I
determined on going to see, to see if need be, the
very devil raised. At the time appointed I was on
my way to the place, not, however, without very
serious misgivings. On arriving there my attention
was arrested by another mammoth poster, flaunting
the inevitable, " Going to raise the devil to-night."
An instinctive dread seized me as if by material
force. Ah!—said an impulse—you have learned
how to *trifle* with God, but you are in *earnest* with
the Devil. Don't back out now, telegraphed another—pay your shilling and go in. Crowds of the
lowest, the most vulgar of London's populace rushed
past me, paid their fee and entered. It was a morti-

fying thought for one with my pride in refinement at least, to be in such company. For some minutes, therefore, I stood tacitly gazing on that awful poster, when my hand involuntarily slipped into my pocket and drew from it a shilling. Starting from the deep reverie into which I had fallen, and goaded by an invisible agent, I burst the barriers of dread and scruple, pushed forward, paid the cost, and actually entered.

Old as I am at this time, the horrible infatuation by which I was propelled, and the dreadful agony of mind in which I found myself on arriving at a seat, are fresh in my imagination. Here I am *in the rotunda*, and the vilest of the vile are my companions —all brought together to hear God denounced, and to see the "devil raised." I had meanwhile walked to the opposite side, being attracted by a small reading desk. I was anxious to see and hear, although I dreaded it. Immense crowds continued to fill up the vast amphitheatre. I looked among them to detect if possible anybody whom I might know; but my sight failed me through fear. I tried to conjecture how the devil was going to be *raised*. Now I fancied it was to be through some magic art: again in the person of one of the chimney-sweepers present. I even gazed with vacant, yet half-expectant glare, at the strange-looking corners, and ugly caricatures about the platform. My imagination was finally so wrought up, that I cried out aloud, "Where am I?" Some one near me answered, "This is the Rotunda, sir." I started at the answer and gazed at the man. Trembling with emotion, I again looked over the

place in its entire extent, my eyes resting upon fully
two thousand human beings of both sexes, and the
very dregs of the city. My pride was fully roused.
I started to my feet to make for the door, when at
the same instant the whole noisy rabble became
suddenly quiet and turned their dirty faces all in one
direction. It took me by surprise. The devil's
coming, I surmised; so I too looked that way. I
saw him! He appeared like a man, wearing a black
silk gown, with something white about his neck,
gloves on, and a book in his hand. My hair arose,
but not to reverence him: it stood on end. My eyes
fastened on him as he stalked and stalked along the
avenue near me. I was dreadfully alarmed. O
God, Lord have mercy on me! *Is* this the devil?
who is it? A filthy scavenger near by answered,
"Its Bob Taylor, zur." I drew a breath. On, on,
on, he stalked, his gown brushing me as he passed.
Another breath—so far, I'm safe.

My eyes, riveted, followed him to the neat, low,
square pedestal whereon he laid the book. Upon
this he placed a white handkerchief, and then, very
ceremoniously clasping his gloved hands together,
turning up the white of his eyes at the same time
and with equal devotedness, he laid his head down
upon the Bible. He continued in this posture several minutes, during which time the silence was
really awful. I looked: I wondered: I trembled.
In fact, all eyes were upon the "devil-raiser." Presently he commenced gesticulating, and, gradually
straightening himself nearly to bending backward,
exhibiting also the palms of his hands, and spread-

ing his fingers widely apart—" I've been praying,"
chuckled he, " as fervently as a parson."

On hearing this, the whole multitude broke out
into a roar of discordant laughter. Well now, methought, I've seen many a better trick at the theatre :
but then he did look so funny as he said it, and I
laughed too. I certainly felt a great disgust for the
" devil-raiser," especially if this is the way he intended to teach the non-existence of God. He has
made but a poor beginning, I inwardly crowed, and
then took comfort in the idea that if his rope breaks,
I can prove my identity with Abraham by the sign
and seal of circumcision, so I will still hang on to
Moses, and be safe, in spite of the devil or his raiser.
Presently he commenced to lecture. He quoted
scripture, held it up in a ridiculous light, and left
the impression thus given. He made the scriptures
apparently contradict themselves, blasphemed at the
idea of a Trinity, (!) defied God, laughed at the
devil, and said that the world was from eternity ; all
things came by chance ; death is the last of man, as
man ; he will thereupon change to some other animal, and will come back either barking, bleating,
squeaking, quacking, or in some other imaginable
way. It was in this odor that his entire speech was
made.

When he had finished, he thanked the *ladies* and
gentlemen for their attendance, and invited us to
come again on the morrow night to hear more. Ah !
reasoned I on leaving, if there is such a being as the
devil, he would certainly have put in an appearance
to-night. Had he not done so, pious reader ?

How readily do the stings of a guilty conscience cease to pain when they are " healed slightly." Although my mind was so thoroughly harrowed up on this occasion, yet when the next night came, it required but little effort to overcome my feelings of fear, and thus gain my own consent to visit this " den of thieves " once more.

The infidel now informed us that " Moses was a liar; Paul was a fool; Christ was a bastard; God is a myth; the Bible is a fable; and man, man is everything!" Well done, I ejaculated, good enough for a " Christian " to talk about. Its taste was so agreeable that I drank it all down. Yes, I swallowed the poison without an effort, and even thought Robert Taylor a wonderful man. Such is the power of sinful attraction, that I continued to hear him frequently; I actually grew to love him and his cause. Yes, my hell-deserving soul did actually *love* the infidel. His sophistry had mastered me. I was overcome; I adored him. I followed up the lectures until I became an adept in infidelity. I now looked upon all religions alike as folly, the Bible a book of lies, Christ a Jewish impostor, God a mere chimera, death an eternal sleep, the resurrection a natural transmigration of matter, and the Judgment-day a mere humbug.

O my ever patient, adorable Lord God, enter not into speedy judgment with me. Remember not against me the sins of my youth, for Jesus' sake. Amen.

For some time past I had not been annoyed at home by the customary surveillance. This was a great relief to me. It happened, however, that one night, returning from the lecture quite late, I found the drawing-room full of company. I was overflowing with "argument," and ready for an encounter. Contrary to my expectations, my father attacked me. "Where have you been to-night, sir; to the theatre?" No sir, to the Rotunda. "What have you been doing there?" Hearing Robert Taylor expose the folly of all the religions in the world. Whack, went the cards with an oath; and as the company continued to whack down the cards, I amused them with my philosophy of religion; I told them all that I knew, and more than they ever knew. I defamed Moses and Christ, laughed at religion and blasphemed God, and then capped the whole by spouting Shakspeare's Seven Stages of Man. Father thought I was growing clever; my brother laughed at me. The ladies, however, turned up their noses, and I have no doubt that the thinking part were utterly disgusted—certainly they should have been. Soon the gaudy party broke up. O, how they swore at each other; and what with charges of cheating, winners laughing, losers mad, the name of God invoked in every oath, which was prefixed with a "by," or a "so help me," it was if not a hell, a bedlam.

I was quite used to hearing it, so it did not move me at all, save that, my infidelity being purer than my Judaism, I now considered swearing *absurd:* I knew no sin in it, or in anything. So I only laughed at them. Keep your tempers, counseled I, it will be all the same in a thousand years.

"It is of the Lord's mercies that I am not consumed, because His compassions fail not."

Time rolled on, and I still felt secure. What harm could ever befall me? I had now secured successively two grand hiding places, "Moses" and Taylor. "Moses" had failed, but I was safe in the "devil-raiser." And when Taylor showed any signs of tottering, I flew back again to "Moses." I was indeed like the troubled sea, throwing up mire and dirt. For me there was no rest. Yet I hated both Christ and Christians worse than ever. Everything within, without, and about me declared that, there is a God. And my own secret convictions consented to that proposition.

> "Where am I? and from whence?
> I nothing know, but that I am;
> And if I am, somewhere there must be a God
> And if a God there is, that God how great!"

"Whither shall I go from Thy spirit? or whither shall I flee from Thy presence? If I ascend up into Heaven Thou art there. If I make my bed in hell, behold Thou art there. If I take the wings of the morning and dwell in the uttermost parts of the sea, even there shall Thy hand lead me, and Thy right hand shall hold me. If I say '*surely* the darkness shall cover me,' even the night shall be light unto me. Yea, the darkness hideth not from Thee, but the night shineth as the day; the darkness and the light are both alike to Thee."

The darkest shades of vice cannot produce an abyss of sufficient depth and density to hide iniquity from the Almighty eye. So I found it. True, I felt secure while I was under the discipline of Taylor. I never once dreamed, but that he could work his way through safely. Yet, deep and dark as was this hiding place, my Father in Heaven saw and cared for me even there. He proved to me that the " reign of the wicked is short;" and He used even this wicked man as a most powerful means of bringing me to the light.

As a stranger to the leadings of God's providence, I had no desire to trace His hand in any event. I felt satisfied in remaining a Jew, or infidel, as best suited my circumstances. Here I slept; and never would I have awakened this side of eternity, " if it had not been the Lord who was on our side when men rose up against us: then they had swallowed us up quick, when their wrath was kindled against us: then the waters had overwhelmed us, the stream had gone over our soul; then the proud waters had gone over our soul. Blessed be the Lord, who hath not given us a prey to their teeth."

Taylor was " raising the devil," all over the city. He seemed to be gaining ground. Infidel clubs were everywhere formed, and we supposed, on solid ground: but how firm in reality, facts will show. The Lord Jehovah threw this atheistic worm upon a bed of affliction. For several days, he struggled, despairing of life. He dreaded death!! He had lain tormented by a burning fever many hours, when suddenly he started up in his bed and shrieked, " O Christ, Christ, Christ! O, that I had a Christ now to fly to! I have gained more converts to the devil in one hour's preaching of infidelity, than I did to

Jesus Christ in a year when I was his accredited minister." Thus confessing, he fell exhausted and gasping upon his pillow. This time he succeeded in effectually "raising the devil." Like wild-fire flew the word all over the nation; Taylor has renounced infidelity: he has invoked, yes invoked Jesus Christ, upon his death-bed. His disciples only sneered. "Taylor," they retorted, "will die like a man." I thought so too, but evidently a very wretched one.

In this extremity, I felt that I was driven into the very labyrinth of perplexity. Infidel clubs were disbanding, and—could I admit it—my rope broke also. After a while, however, Taylor recovered, and —horrible fact—he actually resumed his infidel post again. Doubtless he regained, for the most part, his standing and his disciples. As for me, I could no longer trust to a reputation whose foundation sank at every blast. He wants this very "hanged one," does he? Then good-bye Taylor. So again shifting my position, I denounced the devil-raiser as being a Christian, and once more fell back upon the convenient Israelitish origin as my stronghold. O Moses, whither thou goest, I will go! What thou doest, I will do! What thou thinkest, I will think! Thy God shall be my God! And when I die, the same Hand shall bury me, and I will be hid in the self-same grave. And as for you, father Abraham, I look so much like you, that anybody can tell at first glance, that I am your son. *You* cannot disown me; so I'm safely landed once more, beyond a doubt.

CHAPTER XI.

LOVE'S EPISODE.

It will not be long, dear reader, before you will be able to weld all these links into a chain. Commonly as occurs the heading of this division in both sterner prose and tinselled poetry, I would deem it trifling to treat of it in this narrative, were it not sacredly connected with results about which you are expecting to read. At any rate you will not certainly think the less of my little book because it contains a love story. You will even agree with me, perhaps, that anybody who cannot give some account of love, has no business to write a book. But mark, I do not say the correlative of this.

Brother, who was several years older than myself, had for a considerable time past been paying his addresses to a beautiful, young Jewess, with, however, neither the knowledge nor consent of our father. During the period of two years, the love on both sides was warmly reciprocated. It seems not to have occurred to brother that, there's many a slip between the cup and the lip, and consequently he did not fortify himself against the sad disappointment which befell him. By some mischievous means, my dear, indulgent father obtained information about what was going on. So one day he took

my brother by surprise by asking him whether he
went to see II., and if he wanted to marry her? The
poor boy was frightened—what boy would not be?
He turned pale, and trembling all over, stammered
out, "Y-e-e-e-s." No more was said. Father turned
away abruptly, leaving the petrified chap to dig out
the secret as best he might. . On that very evening
my unsuspecting brother went as usual to visit Miss
II.   During the evening, the young lady's father put
a letter into his hands.   It was written by our own
father, not the hoped-for father-in-law, and directed
to Mr. II.   Of course *I* did not see it, but what I
learned from my brother himself of the contents of
the letter, I feel justified in putting in shape for my
present purpose.   So let us make a palimpsest.

Mr. II.—Sir:

I understand that my son Abraham is courting your daughter, M. I beg leave to inquire of
you whether you intend to give your daughter £500
(five hundred pounds) as her marriage portion? If
not you will please notify my son to discontinue
visiting your house. If, however, he is determined
to marry the girl without that amount of money, I'll
never give him a penny.   (Signed, etc.)

Of course the entire family of the lady felt indignant, and promptly informed my brother that the
best thing he could do would be to go home and
ask his father to go courting for him.   During the
next day my crest-fallen brother was summoned to
appear before the august bar of our honored sire.
"I tell you what it is," remonstrated father, " that

gall's too poor, and if you marry her you may expect
to be a beggar all the days of your life, but if you
get one who is worth five hundred pounds, I'll double it and give you a round thousand. Don't go to
see that poor gall any more." How the poor fellow
received this loving admonition, I must leave the
reader to imagine, as I cannot adequately describe.
The poor fellow cried a whole week without cessation; and for the whole week I tried to make him
angry. I laughed at him, I swore at him, I derided
-him; but all to no purpose. I could not rouse him
by any means whatever. At last I said to him,
" Abe, if I were you, I'd marry M. any how; don't
resign your independence for a few paltry pounds.
If the *old man* won't keep us unless we marry five
hundred pounds, I can play him a trick just about
right. I'm acquainted with a five hundred pound
chance, that I can get at any time. But I know
that the old man won't like my choice. I don't care
for that, I can marry and have a fortune too, independently of him." This speech had the desired
effect. His sorrows now found a tongue, in loud
lamentations. "Thank God," he cried, "that poverty is no sin; if it were, a great many of us would
have to answer for it." Thus he lost his girl, and
thus I was stimulated to make an effort to secure
mine. I must necessarily close this division abruptly, and expect to recur to it again in my next.

CHAPTER XII.

THE TRAPPER IS TRAPPED.

The result of my infidel experience, as overruled, proved to be a future and lasting blessing to my soul. Judaism had taught me to be sectional in my society as well as creed; but infidelity broke that chain of bigotry, and gave me a free ticket to go where I chose and select what society I might prefer. I consequently formed a large and respectable intimacy among Gentiles, which I found to be of so pleasant a character, that I had no disposition to throw it off, even after I had renounced Taylor. Still I was ignorant of the character of that God whose watchful providence was ever with me. "Sentence against *my* evil work" was "not speedily executed," and therefore my wicked heart was "fully set in me to do evil." I gave myself up to every kind of vice and pleasure that could be procured with money. My days and nights were alike spent in profligacy. Led into the haunts of infamy by my brother, and winked at by my father, I arrogated permission to sin against God with impunity.

"Madly I ran the sinful race,
Secure without a hiding place.

Yet the Lord was slow to anger. We "hear the sound thereof but cannot tell from whence it cometh or whither it goeth." But the Lord, who controls the tornado and darts the fury of His eye in the lightning, whose voice is heard in the thunder, and who calleth the stars by their names, who holds the comet in His hand and numbers the stars in the milky way, who upholds universal empire by the word of His power, He, even He knows all things, and overrules them to His own glory.

Little did I think, while blaspheming His holy name, that even then His bowels were moved in compassion for me. Even then He loved me. Alienated as I was from Him, His eye nevertheless was watching over me. He had measured Satan's chain. Nor could he pass over his boundary line. The hand of the enemy was laid heavily upon me, yet he could not touch my life. The cudgel that he raised for my destruction, fell upon his own head and was instrumental in working out my deliverance from his entangling meshes. And if the patient reader will bear with me a little longer, and overlook my imperfections, I will devote the following pages of this book to the history of my introduction into the Zion of Jesus.

When it was decided that my brother must separate himself from the girl he loved, one who possessed beauty, accomplishments and virtue, but not money, and when I saw the effect it had upon his health, a feeling of indignation against my father seized my breast. I rose up upon my supposed superiority, and resolved to take my own course in the matter of my choice for a wife. Mine was a feeling of revenge, and I determined to carry it out.

The boasts that I had made to my brother were founded upon an acquaintance I had formed with a mother and her daughter; the latter an only child, and one who I supposed would be at some future time an heiress. But her history shall be given in its proper place. Thither I bent my steps, being urged forward by a confident expectation of victory over that far, far off five hundred pounds.

As a matter of course, I looked on these two ladies as Christians, simply because they were not of Jewish descent. And here I must confess, that my old prejudice retarded my progress quite disastrously to my cause. In time, however, I ventured to test the possibility or probability of success—a very delicate procedure! I did not exactly "pop the question," but arrived so near to it that *I was caught in the very attempt.* It was too late now for me to back out. She understood me, but did not reply as readily as I anticipated. My pulse beat high, and seemed to say, look out for a squall. In a moment, I entertained serious fears that all my boasting would terminate, minus " five hundred pounds." My suspense lasted only a few minutes, which seemed like so many hours. Then in quite a matter-of-fact, business style, she informed me that she would give an answer in a few days. This much I entered on my credit side.

" A few days." Will they ever expire? How long *must* I wait? O, how long a single week! But I was in moral " durance vile;" I was placed in a situation over which I had no control. Steel teeth seemed to hold me so fast, that I could not extricate myself. I felt that my ærial castle had already vanished away into its constituent atmosphere, and almost resolved not to go back again, to make a fool of myself. But my moral perceptions were like the negro's lump of ice drying by the fire. " The more him dry, the more him wet." The more I wouldn't go back, the more I would. And back I went. I was kindly received by both ladies, and soon seated beside my own five hundred pounds. I felt quite at home. In a few minutes, the young lady commenced to fulfil her promise. In reporting our conversation, L. is lady; M. myself.

L. I don't see, Mr. Davis, how you and I can be married to each other.

M. Why? (with that look of confusion which is no look.)

L. Because there exists so great dissimilarity between us. We are of different religions; and according to your religion, you may not keep company with one of another nation, while, according to my religion, I may not be " unequally yoked with an unbeliever."

Here was argument that I must meet, and delivered too with such firmness that it had a most astonishing effect upon me. I had not visited her to hear *reason*, but having evoked it, I must abide the issue. Surprised, disappointed and vexed, I affected to laugh. But *that* was not argument. Then I tacked about, and invoked Voltaire and Taylor. But the detestable system was abominable, and to her most disgusting. I made the distance greater with every word I said. I had now aroused her keenest sensi-

8

bilities, and she rejected my infidelity with disdain.
She was in possession of a secret of which I was entirely ignorant: *she was a true Christian*. Finding
that I was losing ground rapidly, and was likely to
be repelled by a young lady, I resolved to make one
more desperate effort to save myself. In a moment
I felt as if inspired with the full spirit of infidelity.
Summoning all my remaining courage for the effort,
I made a desperate beginning with a dreadful, blasphemous oath. I was not suffered to proceed, being
checked in an instant by the young lady, with a cutting reproof. "Mr. Davis," she expostulated mildly,
"swearing is neither fashionable, polite nor brave;
it does not become a gentleman." This was more
than I could bear. Mortified in the extreme, and
indignant to overflowing, I arose to leave the room
abruptly. The young lady saw that I was exceedingly chagrined, and not wishing me to leave her
house in so ill humor, judiciously changed the subject, with a very cunningly sweet smile inviting me
to be seated. Some how I could not refuse. But
scarcely had I complied, before she asked me a question which did not set very easily upon my mind.
"Mr. Davis," resumed she, "what has become of
Jerusalem?"

In no way could any mortal have prostrated me
so quickly. All my younger days I had been praying for that identical Jerusalem, and now that a
plain, sensible question is put to me about its history, I'm so ignorant that I cannot answer. Forget-
ting the reproof, I swore again that I did not care
what had become of Jerusalem, that I had a better

country to live in than ever Jerusalem was, if indeed there ever was such a place. The piercing eye that I met, made mine wince. Feeling that I had exposed my ignorance, and had become a victim to my pride and infidelity, before true women, whose minds were imbued with virtue and religion, I became instantly as uneasy as if I had been upon a public examination without preparation, and felt that, could I only see the other side of the street door once more with a sound brain, I should truly rejoice.

Fearing lest I should never get away, I again arose, this time very politely, to make my everlasting exit, when lo, another detention! This time the young lady's mother addressed me. "Is it your intention, Mr. Davis, to continue visiting my daughter?" How, in my frenzy, I wanted to spit fire at her! I wished that she had been in that very Jerusalem before she interfered. But as there was no getting off without an answer, I replied in the affirmative, and moved on toward the door.

In a moment that power of which it is said that it never rests, accosted me again. "Mr. Davis," also spoke up the young lady, seemingly in sprightly jest, "you mustn't come back again unless you can tell me what has become of Jerusalem!" Without making any reply, I turned about and left abruptly, determined, however, never to return. On reaching the open air once more, I drew a long breath—a breath of liberty. Very soon I was seized with a feeling of chagrin and mortification, resulting from the consideration that I had lost my charmingly modest and intelligent—must it come up?—five hundred pounds. When the next day arrived, I was very ill-humored.

Frequently was I admonished " not to bite any-body;" but if there did exist symptoms of hydro-phobia, I am happy to know that I did not hurt a soul. My malady, however, was sorely aggravated by my brother, who after a while, came hurriedly toward me, with his countenance so brightened up that he threw me entirely into the shade. He longed to communicate the pleasing intelligence to me that father had taken a great fancy to E., a rich, young Jewess, and wished that he would go to see her. "I know her," chirped he; "I shall be rich yet; what do you think of that chance, eh?" I was too much embittered to congratulate him, and sourly replied, " Well, if you get her, you get her; and if you miss her, you miss her." I had just enough remaining sense to keep my disappointment a pro-found secret.

Although I had relinquished all ideas of marry-ing, yet I could not lose all interest in the girl who had set me to thinking. But how to resume my visits I was at a loss to know. The past exposure of my ignorance, my ungentlemanly conduct, and above all, my unprepared lesson, all stood before me as so many insurmountable, immovable obstacles. Several days elapsed, and I found that in spite of my effort to be resigned and tranquil, I was in reality considerably disturbed. But I knew the remedy, alas! I must go to Jerusalem for it. It really looked like quite a serious predicament, that I could tell a little about every nation on earth, knew their geography and history, but Jerusalem, to which I have turned my face, and for which been praying for so many years, it was buried so deep in rabbinical mystery, that I could not find its history in all the years of my school training. How I censured my teachers!

However, to work I went in earnest, determined upon arriving at veritable historical facts. I succeeded! I could now answer the standing question, "What has become of Jerusalem?"

Depend upon it, dear reader, that I became a happy youth. With an enlightened mind and a glad heart, I at once resolved upon returning to the centre of all my attraction, feeling fully assured that I should be both forgiven and welcomed back again.

Once more I am on my way to Derby street. As a child who has a message to deliver, continues to say it all along the road, through fear he may forget it upon arriving at the destination, I actually, with every few steps, audibly pronounced "Jerusalem," and before I had quite finished repeating, lo, I was once more in the house of my much-admired—school ma'am.

The ladies seemed glad to see me, and I really felt in a good humor. With a lady's hand in mine, can you wonder that in another minute a nearer approach was gained, that we were seated beside each other? I felt stimulated by an irresistible impulse, constraining me to tell her the whole story of Jerusalem as good-humoredly as if I had never made a fool of myself.

"Now for Jerusalem," started I. The sweet smile of approbation that appeared, encouraged me to go on. By this time I felt even like having a frolic over it. M., discoursed I, if you *want* any information about Jerusalem, I'll tell you all I know about it. Well, let me see; O Jerusalem. Well then, Jerusalem was a city in the land of Canaan. Won't that do? She laughed. Hold on, I'll tell you a little more. Wasn't it the metropolis of Judea? Yes, and it was west of the river Jordan, and east of the Mediterranean sea. It was built on high land, and king Solomon erected a temple there. Now M., won't that suit you? Ragged as my story was, it was received with a condescending pleasure, and you might have seen my countenance brighten at the prospect of regaining those miserably far off "five hundred pounds." In fact, I began to be puzzled which to choose, the girl or her imaginary fortune.

A feeling of exultation took hold of me, and something seemed to say, I've won her. Next minute I was building "castles in the air." Plans for the future were laid out, and others followed in rapid succession. But just as I had arrived at the height of my fancied happiness, behold another mortification, in the form of a question, was laid upon the carpet for my disposal, by the same fair author as the last. "Mr. Davis," observed the beauty, "is it true that Jerusalem existed, and has long since been destroyed; but what has become of your people?" My people! I laughingly responded. I am a Cosmopolite; all people are my people. "True," she chimed in, "all people are by nature on a footing with yourself. But did you not but just now say that your country was destroyed? Now how can there be a nation without a people? Where, therefore, are your nation's people, the Jews?"

Who can imagine my mortification at having such questions pressed upon me, questions which I was so entirely unprepared to answer? I wished that all her questions had been in Jerusalem when the Romans got it, or at the bottom of the sea, or anywhere, rather than where they were, bothering my poor brain. I did try to be modest; I blushed, something rose in my throat. I thought it was my heart. At length I timidly replied, "I suppose they are scattered all over the world."

By this time, I had fairly pushed out into the open sea of perplexity and vexation. I grew impatient to be gone, for I could detect in the peculiar manner of the "missionary," an indication that another question would speedily arrive. My indignation ran high. I looked at her, then at my hat, then at the door, and heartily wished that I had not renewed my visits. My only alternative was to cut my evening visit short as possible. On the impulse of the moment I rose to my feet, seized my hat, and was about to make for the door. In an instant she was on her feet also, and standing by my side, "Don't be in a hurry, Mr. Davis, I *do* want to ask you another question." Her manner was so lady-like, and withal fascinating, that I could not move, though in my heart I cursed this catechism. I paused, trembled, bit my lip; but ere I was aware, I was safely re-seated on a chair by the side of my would-be deliverer. "Mr. Davis," sighed she, "I feel very much interested in behalf of your nation. Do you know the reason for which God permits your people to be scattered all over the world?" I was too indignant to reply with common civility. "You are more interested for my nation than I am; I neither know the cause, nor do I care to." At this she expressed great surprise. What! could I, a Jew, feel so little concern for the welfare of my people, while *Christians* were so much concerned for them. I must here confess that I thought the same in view of her immediate and individual anxiety, but beyond her, all the world was a blank. "Let me tell you," insinuated she, "about the grand, moral cause of the downfall of your nation. When our Saviour, Jesus Christ, was arraigned before Pontius Pilate by your people, for no offence against either the laws of Heaven or earth, Pilate declared that he found no fault in Him, and would have released Him; but your people were vehement in their cries against Him that He should be crucified, even declaring that they would rather let loose in the community a common robber, who had been fairly tried, found guilty and condemned for sedition and murder. Pilate then asked, What shall I do to your king? Your people then flew in the face of their own law, and cried, We have no king but Cæsar. Now, Cæsar was not a Jew. Still Pilate tried to reason with the crowd, and to plead for His release. But your people were mad in their cries for His crucifixion. So Pilate passed the unjust sentence of death upon the cross. Then as a token of his disapproval of the whole proceeding, he took water and in the presence of your nation washed his hands, averring, I am innocent of the blood of this just person; see ye to it. And your people with one voice cried out, Let his blood be upon us and on our children."

She would have said more, but violent emotions choked her utterance, her lip quivered, her voice failed, her beautiful eyes filled with tears, and she turned her head aside to give vent to her feelings. I saw the tears fall fast: but did not understand anything about it. I was petrified. I could do no more than gaze at her, not knowing which to admire most, her beauty or her eloquence.

It will not be a difficult task for the reader to picture in his mind's eye the scene before us. There were but three of us in the room. The mother, who had been looking on and hearing in silence, showed signs of the intense interest she took in the matter. The daughter, broken down with emotion, buried her lovely face in a handkerchief. And I, fairly palsied by this last speech, even to dumbness, sat for a moment wondering how she knew all this. Yet I dare not, as I grew sensible again, either ask or reply. The sting of prejudice goaded me. I felt insulted by those words, "Our Saviour." To me they were hateful. I thought I would have received a poisoned dagger in my breast sooner than to have heard that name, Jesus Christ, especially under such circumstances and in such connection, uttered in my presence. I could hear a Jewish rabbi or an infidel as Taylor, and laugh. But who is this—" Our Saviour?" Not mine! I hate Him!

I looked long and steadily, however, at the weep-

ing girl and her mother, scrutinizing them alternately in utter amazement. I could endure no
more. A mountain of my Jewish hatred rushed
into my distracted brain. Mechanically I seized my
hat, and rushed out of the house, leaving the faithful daughter of the Lord, and her mother, wondering
after me. The open air once gained, I hurried away
from the abode of Christians, nor did I slacken my
pace until I quite reached my own private room,
where, between Moses and Taylor, quiet to my distracted mind was once more restored.—This last
visit gave me such offence, that I resolved to put a
a wide distance between us forever.

It is time now that I give my reader a little history
of this Christian lady. She was one of a small family of brothers and sisters. Distance and death had
removed all from the mother's side, save this one.
Her father was living in affluence, but having embraced infidelity many years before, he carried out
its principles in his life, by deserting his wife, having
allowed whom a separate maintenance, he now roved
at large, in open defiance of the Lord of creation.
The Christian influence of the mother was reflected
resplendently in the character of the daughter.
Thus they lived alone for each other and for Christ.
When the mists were removed from my eyes, and I
lived to rejoice in Christ Jesus my Saviour, I learned
all I now write of her history. So great was the
agonizing anxiety of this child of grace for her father's salvation, that she would way-lay him in his
walks, throw herself at his feet in the open street,
and implore him, with her womanly eloquence, to

turn to the Lord and live. Often has she told me that at such times her father would raise her up, throw himself upon her bosom, and weep aloud. Sometimes he would cry, " O my daughter, nothing makes me feel but your tears." Then he would thrust a purse of gold in her hand, kiss her tenderly, and tear himself away.

O Infidelity! this is your very fairest production. " Jesus wept." Alas, for whom ?—Christian woman, your loved ones about you are ungodly; let them see a tear drop from your eye; make them to know that it falls unbidden, irrepressible in their behalf. It may harden their hearts apparently for a while, as it did my own. But a woman's tears and prayers rise high before the throne of Jehovah. They cannot plead in vain.

CHAPTER XIII.

STRUGGLING TO GET FREE.

The experience of life covers a great variety of incidents. Some of these appear to be of very small importance, yet each plays its part distinctly. And God, who overrules all things for the promotion of His own glory, connects importance with the most trifling circumstance, that it may become subservient to His own will. Eminently true is this with reference to our conversion to God. He does not employ the mighty of this world to carry out His plans; but the weak things of earth, in His hand, are "mighty to the pulling down of strongholds." 2 Cor. x: 4.

This is proven true in my life. Has it not also in yours? It is necessary, therefore, that I take my leave of these two pious women for the present, in order that I may show you what effect the last-named interview had upon me.

On arriving in my room, I immediately retired to my bed, "seeking rest but finding none." A strange, restless drowsiness crept over me, and M.'s form appeared. Standing before me, she addressed me with her wonted eloquence. Once more I saw her earnest manner, her brimming eye, her quivering lip, her choked utterance. Once again I heard those

strange, strange words, Let His blood be upon us
and on our children. I groaned and turned upon
my pillow; but could not conjecture what all this
uneasiness meant. The restless night was followed
by a troubled morning. I was weary in mind. The
family noticed that there was something wrong, but
not venturing to express an opinion positively as to
my ailment, they resorted to guessing a hundred
things in turn the matter with me. But no one
guessed it had to do with *the blood of Christ.* I certainly did not. Yet so it was. True, I felt mortified to think how I had lost my imaginary prospect
for life. But beyond this, it did not seem to trouble
me. That mysterious speech rather constantly
sounded in my ears, "Let His blood be upon us
and on our children." To say the least, my peace
was actually disturbed, nor could I find a quietus in
anything but the excess of wine and London amusements. Wine-drinking to excess, and amusements
of London!

I did not then know that He, whose blood was
staining me, had said that no gate of the underworld
should ever prevail against His church. Little did
I think that I had entered into the broadest of them
all; and nothing prevented me from advancing, but
the utter impossibility of discovering the "blood of
Christ" upon that road. I was verily blood-dyed,
but did not know it. The Lord, in His own time
and manner, revealed it to me.

The comedy of the theatre failed to excite my
laughter. That awful language rang in my ear;
and that still more awful denunciation, which my

people invoked upon themselves, impressed my mind with a sense of horror. "Can it be," whispered my doubt, "that Jesus Christ is so bad a character as the Jews represent Him." Is he an impostor, a bastard, an evil angel, a blasphemer, cursed of God; and have my people really invoked the curse of such a character? Horrid enough to invoke the curse of a good being, but to call for a lasting curse "upon us and on our children," from such a character as Jesus Christ, is dreadful. I trembled, realizing that the "blood of Christ" was against me in that playhouse.

As calm follows storm, so after I had quit the theatre for that night, I reflected upon the cause of the spoiling of my enjoyment. But storms followed hard on. Maddened at my disappointment I at once resolved to erase from my mind every feature of that female preacher, and also those hateful words that haunted me. All my energies were summoned for the task. I laughed, swore, blasphemed, and satirized. I resorted to places of amusement and danced. I swallowed liquor and gambled. Yet wherever I went, whatever I did, I saw "His blood" everywhere and always. Then I gathered together a number of novels, obscene books and ballads. I tried to read them. But on every page there appeared to be large blots of blood. All day long I thought of "His blood." In the night, my restless sleep was disturbed by dreams of the past. There stood that womanly messenger, weeping and repeating to me, "His blood be upon us and on our children."

This condition of things soon drove me to a terrible conclusion. Surely, soliloquized I, if there is any truth in what is attributed to my people in calling for "His blood upon us and on our children," the Almighty must have said "amen" to it! I too am then stained with it; nor can I erase it. Thus each day my gloom increased; I knew not why, but I could not enjoy a tranquil hour.

This frame of mind had continued several weeks, when an idea started up within me. Have I ever heard a *substantial* argument counter to the idea of the Messiah having been upon this earth, appearing in the person of any one? This seemed to arouse my conscience from a deep lethargy. I thought about it a moment only, and answered with a decisive "No." I could remember nothing but thread-bare fables. After all, I began to admit, *perhaps* the Messiah may have come. And now if He has actually been upon this earth, I want to know the fact; and know it I will! But what chance had I to learn? Whom could I ask? I had shut myself out from inquiry by an avowal of infidelity. If I should fall back upon Judaism, bigotry and prejudice were an eternal barrier. If I inquired of Christians, I knew what would be their uniform reply. Besides, I greatly feared the Jews. So I resolved to assume the attitude of a candid but independent investigator, and ask no assistance from any living being.

My first resolve was to receive the Old Testament scriptures as truth. I at once discarded Taylor and all his parrot-like, blasphemous buffoonery. I then engaged to read Moses and the Prophets fairly, honorably, and impartially. I marked every passage of importance, that I thought *must* refer to the Messiah O, that I had then known how to pray. What a glorious teacher I should have had. But alas, my soul was barren, dead. How could I arrive at an understanding of the sacred scriptures, having no man to explain to me? I had no books to guide me and no prayer to offer. Still, Jehovah was my secret Helper.

The first place at which I paused, was Genesis iii. 15: "And I will put enmity between thee and the woman, and between thy seed and her seed; *it* shall bruise thy head and thou shalt bruise *his* heel."

Here I paused and laughed at the idea of enmity between the woman and young serpents. Very natural, for a woman to hate snakes either young or old. But then what does this mean, "*It* shall bruise thy head, and thou shalt bruise *his* heel?" Where shall I locate these two pronouns so as to make them agree in *gender* with the nouns for which they stand?

The seed of the serpent was to be *one of the neuter* gender, whereas that of the woman should be one of *masculine* gender. Who is he? A man?—Pass on! mistrusting mind.

I then came to Genesis xlix. 10: "The sceptre shall not depart from Judah, nor a lawgiver from between his feet until Shiloh come; and unto *him* shall the gathering of the people be." Here again I found a personal pronoun. Is he the "seed of the woman?" If so, is he Shiloh? I remembered that, while yet at school, I learned from several rabbinical authorities, that these passages referred to Messiah. This much, therefore became settled. But, Rabbi

Gerson affirms, "Shiloh has not yet come." He has, moreover, proved this assertion by his famous " big river" story. However, I choose now to think and reason for myself. If Shiloh is Messiah, and he has not come, then Judah as a tribe possesses the sceptre and lawgiver to this day. But where is Judah? Here I confess that I took refuge behind some of the rabbins, and affected to believe that for some special purpose, the Lord had Judah in a secret place. But here started another difficulty. Where are the sister tribes? I could not tell. Still another difficulty was here interposed. The sceptre and lawgiver were never intended for the *exclusive* benefit of Judah, but were simply to *spring* from her, for the benefit no less of the *whole body*—" unto him shall the gathering of the *people* be." But who are *the* people? Does it mean the Jewish nation? Certainly not, they are rather *scattered.* Then, can it mean the Gentile peoples? If so, " His blood" is " upon us and on our children." How can I arrive at facts? Conscience suggested, *by facts.* What facts? Those which point you to the existing reality that *all* the people of the world are gathering unto him, and are becoming Christians. Again those who declare to us that " the combined numbers and wealth of my people throughout the world" is meant, cannot produce either " sceptre" or " lawgiver." The point settled, therefore, was, that these had departed. But when, I could not tell.

My reader doubtless bears in mind that it is not the design of this little book to *prove* any question. In fact, no question for discussion will be started. I

9

merely state what appeared to *me* as truth, when I
was honestly investigating the scriptures for it, with
no other helps than two copies of the *Old* Scriptures,
the one in Hebrew, the other, one of King James'
English Bibles, without the later testament however.
I cannot, therefore, find room to state more than
the fact that upon examining the prophesies, I found
they contained very important matter that rabbis
never read in the ears of the public. I will only
speak of the wicked omission of the three last verses
of the fifty-second chapter of Isaiah, and the whole of
the fifty-third out of the portion to be read, called
" Haphtora." When I read them, and saw there
before me that wonderful prophecy of such a divine
mystery as could not refer to any living being but
the " Shiloh," Messiah; and for the first this flashed
upon me, of which the whole congregation is ignorant, ignorant even that it exists, I blushed for the
dishonesty of the rabbins. This feature was dark,
while the prophecy itself appeared most plain, that
I was compelled in candor to admit that here at
least existed a grievously black spot. I exclaimed,
" Shame to the rabbins for misleading the people."
My education had never referred me clearly to the
fact that the prophesies even bore a general reference
to the Messiah. These were always garbled and
glossed over. But what boy would care about discussion? I did not. Now I wake up to see that the
sacred pages are full of the one great theme—Messiah and Messiah's reign.

Here I fell into a train of reflections. I put modern Judaism in one scale and infidelity in the other.

And while I found no God really in either system, in point of common liberality, that of Taylor, who invited and courted, at least in appearance, both investigation and discussion, was the more weighty of the two. I did not by this award infidelity more praise, but declared that Judaism deserves less. Thus I continued to study The Book, becoming daily more nearly satisfied, that Messiah had come. Still, I wanted more light. I traveled toward the East for it. Once I had faced the East with my eyes shut like a rabbi, simply because Jerusalem was there. But now all the powers of my mind face the rising sun, and my eyes are wide open, lest I should lose one little ray of light. And when the intervening cloud gathered too darkly, I slapped my forehead with impatience, crying, " O, that I could only dare to ask father."

It is with difficulty that I restrain my pen from giving the reader the result of my laborious investigations of the sacred prophets. Everywhere I lighted upon startling disclosures, of different dates, by various persons, looking down through coming time to but one terminus, the appearance of some one person on the earth to be connected in some way with the royal family of David ; one whose existence was to be mysterious, running along from his conception by a " virgin " to his grave with " the wicked." I noted also the wonderful harmony between Moses and Isaiah. Through the former we have mentioned, The seed of the *woman*, rather than of the man : by the latter it is said, A *virgin* shall conceive. I observed also the exalted relation he was

to sustain to the one everlasting, all-glorious Jehovah. In time, my rude notes swelled to a volume.
I could not investigate more. I had enough to con-
vince me that at some past period, in some one mysterious person, Messiah had certainly appeared upon
earth. But in whom, and when? aye, that is the
question. In Jesus of Nazareth, "the hanged one,
the hated?" No, never! My soul recoiled from
the idea. Shuddering, I closed my eyes, bowed my
head, and then inwardly repeated, "Hear, O Israel,
Jehovah our God is one Jehovah."

Supposing that nothing more could be done, I
closed the book. Days and nights of profound meditation followed. I was not satisfied as yet. There
were facts as to time given by the prophet Daniel,
which my ignorance could not comprehend. I resolved, however, to try again. Opening the book of
Daniel at the ninth chapter, and dwelling long and
studiously on the latter part, especially from verse
twenty to the end of the chapter, I at last reached
results that astonished me. If my dear reader is at
all interested in this narrative, he will certainly be
willing to pause here, open his Bible, and read the
verses of Daniel to which I have referred. I discovered, on studying them, that a great and conclusive
work was to be accomplished by the Messiah in person, and within a specified time, its commencement
dating (verse 25) "from the going forth of the com-
mandment to restore and to (re)build Jerusalem."
After searching the books of Ezra and Nehemiah a
long time, I found difficulty in locating the *beginning*
of the seventy weeks on account of the fact that

there were as many as four different decrees or "commandments."

Here I was interrupted by peculiar emotions, in view of my situation. What must be my position hereafter, if all these events have taken place, and Messiah has been "cut off for the people?" O that I could locate the beginning at some late period, so as forever to settle the question in favor of Judaism, appearing as it then would that the Messiah has not yet come. Twist and dodge as I managed to do, the date in question would not go lower down than the fourth, or last decree to build the city and the walls. There I *must* commence the seventy weeks. (See Neh. i: 1–9.)

The next question was as to the period of time to be consumed by the seventy weeks. I knew that prophetically a day stood for a year, (see Numbers xiv: 34,) which gave me the full period of four hundred and ninety years, or seven times seventy from the last decree. What could I now do but look at facts as they are. Every letter of that prophecy relative to my people is truthfully fulfilled; then why not couple these stubborn facts with that to which they claim to belong, namely, with the appearing and cutting off of Messiah himself? Shades of Rabbi Ben Joseph, help me out of this dilemma. But the echoing voice from the tomb replies, "Moses and the Prophets." My head reeled in the face of mathematical evidence like this. Nor am I giving the whole of my research; only what I then obtained. Either Messiah must have come long, long ago, or Daniel was a false prophet. Now that Daniel is a

true prophet of the Lord is evidenced by the fact
alone, that the daily sacrifice has ceased, because the
temple is no more and Jerusalem is in the hands of
strangers. More than once in days past, had I inquired, How long is it since our people discontinued
offerings? One answer came: " A long, very long
time; the Almighty has been angry with us nearly
2000 years." When I remembered this, hearing
Daniel declare as well that Messiah must come *before*
sacrifices and offerings should cease, *before* the destruction of the temple and city, I would do naught else
than conclude that Messiah has certainly come. In
vain I looked about me to escape. I felt the force of
that woman's recital, "Let His blood be upon us and
on our children." Whose blood? Not Christ's,
surely.

Agonizing to ward off the truth that some time
must be fully admitted, I lived as though a sword
was hanging in the air over my head, threatening
momentary destruction. I dreaded to look any
longer through this God-given telescope, lest I
should bring still distant facts near my eye, and so
destroy whatever remained of my frail argument.
But unable to resist the increasing desire to know
the truth, I continued my investigation, only, however, to expose the rottenness of modern Judaism,
and to bring to light with still greater force the truth,
that Messiah has certainly come.

The shock which this ever-brightening discovery
gave my constitution was astonishing. My countenance, naturally pale, began to assume a doleful aspect. All the family noticed it, yet in their igno-

rance of facts, imputed it to any cause but the right one. My pen cannot describe the actual torment of mind in which I was plunged. In vain did I attempt to resist the conviction that Messiah had been upon the earth very many years ago. Still, I could not, I would not admit that "the Christian's god" was he. And if at any time I dare indulge a suspicion of the bare probability that it might be so, it was like signing my own death warrant! The only promising refuge left me was to indulge a hope that I might still find the Messiah in the person of one of the old prophets. But, O, those invulnerable facts set forth by these very prophets—A spotless lamb— Dumb to the slaughter—Born of a virgin—Death ignominious—His grave with the rich and wicked —Himself poor, but called the mighty God—His soul satisfied with seeing His travail; and so, very much more, all uttered *by* these old prophets, and attributed to some one else—marvels of marvels! I could not find such wonders exemplified in any person within the bounds of my limited readings—could others produce a parallel?

Sometimes reason would interpose in behalf of truth. Can you any longer resist the proof of the Messiahship of Jesus of Nazareth upon Judaical premises? Can you longer reject Him by virtue of your old one-sided argument? Conscience cried, 'No. Still, I could not receive Him, because I did not know Him. Neither felt I any desire in that direction. I had never read the " Christian's book," and had no wish to do so. In fact, my mind was crowded with Jewish fables, portraying this same

Christ in such hideous proportions, that I could not
so easily divest myself of them, tack about, and give
him credit for the dozens of fine things that the prophets said about Messiah.　No, no; it will never,
never answer!　So, once again I invoked the old
prophets, and involuntarily exclaimed aloud, Come
David, come Solomon, pray show me that one or the
other of you will answer the character sought apart
from " Christ."　David is the first to reply.　" They
pierced my hands and my feet."　How, crucified?
But *David* was not crucified.　Solomon interposes, *I*
finished my work on earth long before the work of
my temple was completed.　Here Daniel's voice is
recognized.　" In the midst of the week He shall
cause the sacrifice and oblation to cease."　Who
shall do this thing?　Christ?　Impossible!

In vain I tried to settle down in quiet ignorance.
My sleep would be broken up at night, as through
it came a voice sepulchral, " His blood be upon us
and on our children."　Thus my days and nights
were a perpetual torment.　At length I became the
victim of deep mental anguish, which was so apparent that I was the butt and laughing stock of all who
were in the house, who called into service their utmost hilarity to deliver me from my mental throes.
O, that I had then known *how to pray*.　I would have
disburdened my soul of many a load.　But, alas! I
was a stranger to both prayer and the God who
hears it.

Notwithstanding all this trial of mind, steadily
was increasing my anxiety to find out who other
than Christ, this Messiah could be.　Many a time

STRUGGLING TO GET FREE.

while reading the prophecies, I would pause in bewilderment, and cry out, "Who *is* this wonderful person, recognized under so many different names? Can I ever find on the page of history, a person who is able to concentrate them all in himself? If such an one can be produced, he, without a doubt, will be the true Messiah. Again a voice would have it that Jesus of Nazareth is he. Then starting from a deep thought, I hastily contradicted, No, he is not; he cannot be; he is a bastard, an impostor, "the hanged one." Thus I concluded that it was impossible that such a common character could be the Messiah—yes, literally impossible.

Here, a train of thought, ethical in character, began to exercise my mind: thought, too, well calculated to shut me out forever from Christ as my Saviour.

The Law of Moses, teaching the doctrine of retaliation for injuries received, rose up before me, as presenting an insurmountable difficulty. Being ignorant of the New Testament, I very naturally reasoned thus: What if Jesus of Nazareth is the true Messiah, and I become cognizant of that fact; will He not do to me as I have done and still am doing to Him? Most certainly He will. Here the Law roared out, "'Tis *just* that he should." Then, I responded, I will forever remain in ignorance of Him: while I'm ignorant I'm safe, but should I ever become acquainted with Him, and He treats me as I have treated Him, then neither Moses nor Abraham will avail anything for me; I shall be damned forever. There is no mercy for me. Imagining that this reasoning was well-grounded, I tried to be quiet. But quiet I could not be. I do not even now know how to account for it, but with an out-gush of tears, I wept for very agony of soul. I wished that I had never been born, or that Messiah had not been foretold.

The most successful awakener of due appreciation of large benefits enjoyed, is found to be the experience we have after we have lost them. O, how I longed for a friend, to whom I might communicate my thoughts and feelings. Hundreds of human beings daily flit like phantoms past me. Is there among them all one solitary friend? If I could find but one in this time of need, I should be happy. Yet not one dare I trust, unless perchance M. herself might be in the crowd. Yes, I can trust her now, but no one else. Could I now have her by my side, I would repose confidence in her, and to her I would unburden my whole heart. But I dare not venture " there " again. My own bad conduct had shut the door in that direction. True, pride rose high against the thought of again hearing about " His blood," yet I would have endured even that, if through it I could have found the true Messiah. Alas, I have sacrificed that friend. Henceforth I must live in ignorance without her.

Time passed by, leaving me a willing but ignorant slave in the hands of Satan, to be spell-bound more firmly by his powerful delusions. My desire for pleasure, however, was checked, so that my health became so much impaired as to excite the alarm of our family physician. No doubt he was right in his

conjecture as to my physical ailment. He said that
my liver was deranged: but Dr. Kish doubtless
meant—my heart. He gave me a lump of blue-mass
to make into pills, and so be swallowed. I looked
at myself in the glass, and concluded that I was blue
enough without his pills, so throwing away the
mass, I concluded that he too was ignorant of my
malady. Alas, Dr. Kish could not help me.

At length the family became tired out and vexed
with me, because they could not arouse me from my
continual gloom; finally they left me alone, without
doctor, without a friend, to eke out a most miserable
existence. The enemy of God and man took advantage of my weakness, and presented to my already
terrified imagination the most discouraging picture
that the father of lies could invent; so that I concluded that nothing could possibly save me from
eternal death itself. Thus for several days I groaned
between two dark clouds. If Christ is the Messiah,
I shall be damned for the wrong I have done Him.
But if Messiah is some other man, I shall be damned
for my ignorance of him.

Thus I was drifting with the current toward the
awful vortex. Insanity would doubtless have been
my ultimate condition, but for the timely deliverance
of my ever-blessed Saviour, who sent me relief when
I least expected it, and in a manner that, to this late
day and forevermore, will fill my unworthy soul with
devout love and gratitude.

CHAPTER XIV.

THE BATTLE RAGING.

Many years ago I learned that none of God's arrangements, certainly none of the godly man's life, comes by chance. Like all other true Christians, I have since been led to watch the hand of Providence, and have found that I have never been in want of a hand of Providence to watch. Earlier in life, however, these peculiar providences appeared to me purely as accidents, and I treated them as such. Were they, in consequence, any less God's providences? Surely thus far I had had abundant reason to praise the Lord, for leading me along a path so exactly suited to my condition.

Having therefore no other word that I can command, to set forth the ideas that then absorbed me, I must say that one day I was more than usually gloomy. I walked about the house, "seeking rest but finding none." It "happened" that in my wanderings, I suddenly found myself down stairs in the Gentile servants' kitchen. It was no place for me, but the two women being absent, I must forsooth open a dresser drawer. I needed nothing and sought for nothing. Yet there was something that the Lord intended me to have. There lay a book. I must needs open it at the first chapter of the general epistle of James. I stood before the open drawer and read the chapter through. Filled with surprise, I trembled at reading an account of my own condition, especially in a strange book.

Naturally enough, the title page was referred to; when, to my confusion, I read, "The New Testament of our Lord and Saviour Jesus Christ." This is the "Christian's book," I exulted. In a moment it came into my heart to *steal it.* Instantly I obeyed the impulse, and speedily put it into my pocket. A sense of guilt overcame me; fear of detection seized my coward heart. Fancying I heard some one at work in an adjoining cellar, I hurriedly turned from the open drawer, and to the extent of my strength, ran up stairs, taking two and three steps at a time; nor did I stop until I safely entered my bed room. Being perfectly exhausted, I sat down to recover, only however to find myself plunged in a fearful dilemma. I actually owned (?) a "*New* Testament." I did not love it, nor want it; yet I had an irrepressible inclination to read it, if only to show up the falsity of Christianity. There was, however, a difficulty in the way, as my brother lodged in the same room with me, while for me to be detected reading something new, and *such* a book, would have resulted to me disastrously. Sometimes I was disposed to return the book secretly to its place. To part with it altogether, was now out of the question. I must read for myself. I must for myself see what kind of people these Christians are. I must know for myself of what their religion consists. Swayed by motives sometimes honest and sometimes dishonest,

I resolved upon hiding the doubtful treasure until I could find a fair chance to read it privately. It was not long before I had my plans arranged, only awaiting maturity; to this they soon attained.

My father had a large manufacturing establishment about two miles from our dwelling, for the safety of which it was necessary to have somebody sleep upon the premises. A boy whom we called Tom, had for some time past lodged there alone. Here was my chance. So I proposed to my father, that for the better security of the place, I should take up my night's quarters at the warehouse. To this proposition he readily acceded, and the same night I became the companion of Thomas. I soon found that it was necessary to get rid of him, and he being glad to be relieved, did not delay to leave me to myself.

The reader doubtless imagines that in all this manœuvering, I was really actuated by the very purest motive. I blush to confess that the very reverse was the fact. True, I had a strong desire to read the forbidden book, but I did not expect to find in it truth, or anything congenial to my feelings. What I actually expected to discover, was a tissue of absurdities, so grossly idolatrous that just such a head as mine (replenished as it suddenly became with " Bob Taylor, the devil-raiser ") would be sufficient to explode the entire Christian religion. My bones and Jewish reputation were in equal jeopardy. Mine was a deed of darkness. I must be alone.

For a long time the poor servant girl was greatly

troubled for the loss of her testament. Whatever may have been her suspicions about it, she did not once imagine that I was the thief; consequently I continued to have and to hold undisputed possession until future events ripened, the record of which will reveal under what circumstances I ultimately returned it to her. There is a separate interesting fact in this connection, which I have some delicacy in speaking of, through fear you may think I give it here for the mere effect. It is not so. I tell it because it has been on my mind from that time to the present. The names of the two women were Mary and Martha. I do not know that they were any relation to each other. It was *Mary's* Testament I appropriated to myself.

I was now burning for battle. The first business on hand, therefore, was to fortify myself with argument, that then I might go again to visit M. and tell her more about Jerusalem than she ever knew. I would attack her religion in retaliation, she having made an inroad upon mine.

In nervous excitement I carelessly opened the book at the eighth chapter of John. The former part of the chapter made me so angry that I was goaded on to burn the book. No, no, I can't do that, I *must* read more. The part appeared to be nothing but an accumulation of such nonsense as made me think I should have no difficulty in rooting up Christianity out of the earth. Reasonable as it doubtless appears, that no thinking being could possibly understand this or any other book through so much prejudice against it, yet I continued to read

detached portions as likely to furnish me the only
material I wanted. Thus I dwelt on the fifty-first
verse: "Verily, verily I say unto you, if a man keep
my sayings he shall never see death." Ha, ha, ha.
Don't these Christians die as well as Jews? Certainly they do. Is not that fact an evidence that
they don't "keep" his sayings? Then I ask, is
there any Christian religion in existence? I reply,
"No." So without the least serious reflection, without even considering what I was doing, I trium-
phantly closed the book, exulting in my fancied con-
quest.

On the next day I resolved to go at once to visit
the girl preacher, throw down the gauntlet, open the
combat, strike the first blow, (and the last one too,)
belch forth my anti-speeches abruptly in the face of
M., fight valiantly with my fifty-first verse, tell her,
too, that the Jews were right in saying that its author was "mad" and that he "had a devil," prove
to her the consummate folly of her religion, and so
overturn the whole scheme. Certainly!

Confident of success, in the afternoon I sallied
forth, like Saul of Tarsus, to seek the residence of
these Christians, and defeat them with their own
weapons. The book in my pocket, with only two
places read, and at the second a leaf well turned
down, I arrived most valiant at the house. Never,
either before or since this adventure, has my bosom
been inspired with higher confidence of success.
And never have I been so miserably defeated and
completely beaten off my track, as at this time. On
arriving at the door, I raised the knocker. No sooner

was the sound of this heard than I was seized with such an indescribable throbbing in my left side, that I would have given all the world rather than to have embarked upon so unequal a contest. I could not now retire, for the door was quickly opened by the mother herself. There I stood, pale, trembling, and speechless. She invited me in, and to be seated. But once there, in the presence of these two holy women, not a word could I say. I was utterly unable to carry out my plans. If my confusion could be aggravated, it was by the smiling face of M. I hated her for her religion's sake, and for the trouble into which she had plunged me. There I sat, dumb, confounded, a victim of my own madness. I knew, because I felt, that Jehovah, God Almighty was fighting against me.

An interval of several minutes of quiet confusion ensued, which I occupied by looking at my feet. Such conduct was too eccentric to escape the close scrutiny of the ladies. They appeared to be struck with astonishment. At last I was relieved by the maternal voice of the elderly lady falling upon my ear most kindly: "Mr. Davis, what is the cause of your uneasiness?" I could not resist this pleasant, motherly appeal; so in smothered voice I slowly answered, I'm in trouble. After this there followed a very long and perfectly silent pause. At length the same lady again spoke up. "Mr. Davis, of whatever nature your trouble is, I assure you that you may find comfort in the Christian religion." This language aroused me from my stupor. I remembered my errand, and clapped my hand upon the book that

10

was in my pocket. But before I had time to reply, she continued in so kind a manner, " Would you not like to visit a Christian church, one Sunday ?" That was enough. Madam, I indignantly replied, you insult me. I have never been in such a place, and I'll take care that I am never found there in future. Chagrined as I felt, I could but grasp my hat and say good-bye.

Something must have accelerated my motion, for I arrived home in an incredibly short time. There I sat, a victim to pride and prejudice, and withal completely humbled at my failure. A word has not lost its truthfulness because it may have become trite. So, as a burned child dreads the fire, I dreaded to have anything more to do with that mysterious book. Taking it out of my pocket, therefore, I determined upon reading it no more. Still I could not get my own consent to part with it. I did not at that time know why, but I have learned since. The remainder of the week passed away, and with it, I supposed, the whole controversy.

On the following Saturday night, I retired at my usual hour, and soon fell asleep. About midnight I was suddenly aroused, by what I never knew. In a moment I was as wide awake as if I had not been sleeping before. Being alone, I had a fair chance to think over passing events. Presently something suggested that I get up, dress myself, and go to a Christian church. Nobody had insulted me this time by the proposition; but it did seem so strange that such an impression should possess me, that I lay until day-break, my curiosity rising higher all the time. Finally it reached such a pitch, that I determined to go at all hazard, and see for myself what the Christians did there. But here a difficulty presents itself, and one which I cannot set aside. I am expected at home for breakfast. Shall I go? If I do, I must join the family in a Sunday stroll. I must close the day in an aristocratic tea-garden. Well this is all good enough for me: but to church I *must* go, yes, this very day. I looked at all the difficulties, and at once determined to surmount them, and go to " church" without breakfast.

The bells soon announced the time; but *where* should I go, out of the multitude of churches? A number of people, moving in one direction, seemed to invite my company. I followed them to a place of " worship."

Fear of detection prompted me to remain outside. There I amused myself by peeping in every time the door was opened, my curiosity continuing on the increase. At last, the house being filled, the door was left wide open. The interior of the place, in short the entire affair appeared to be very modest. It was a dissenter's chapel. I was not then quite so badly afflicted with deafness as now, and therefore I could and did listen to the singing with satisfaction. But when the minister prayed, I gazed strangely at him, my mouth wide open. Can tongue of mortals describe my surprise, when I heard him pray so feelingly, so fervently, and in tears, (I saw them fall) that " God would convert the Jews." An instantaneous impression seized me, favoring the idea that if this man means any good by his prayer, he at least cannot hate the Jews quite so badly as I have always imagined that the Christians do. Prayer ended, I heard another song; and then the minister proposed to read the eighth chapter of John. In a moment I moved back. Something seemed to say to me, " run, run."

No, I won't run! I'm too proud for that act: I must see the end. So, calling to my assistance all my fortitude, I resolved to hear patiently all that I could under the circumstances. He now announced his " text " to be in the same chapter, commencing at the forty-eighth verse and running to the end of the chapter. I stood as one petrified. (I did not know the ways of the Lord.) Presently he read the fifty-sixth verse, and I thought he looked directly in my eye. In alarm I started back, cursing the Christian in my heart. There now, thought I, that old hag and her daughter are nothing better than witches; they have told the preacher of my past week's trouble upon this very subject.—I thought that the whole thing was gotten up to persecute me because I was a Jew. Yet wonderful as it may appear, I could not retire! I *must* hear it out. The theme was, " The controversy between Jews and Christians." Jesus Christ in the character of the Eternal God, both undertype and as antitype, was most beautifully touched upon and briefly treated of. I had heard argument. Here was a basis for thought I did think, but my heart was so hard; I turned away.

The congregation was at last dismissed. A more wretched mortal than I surely never lived. I turned toward home with a murmuring soul. "His blood" kept pace with me. Conscience whispered, Christ is the true Messiah, the eternal God, The glorious I Am. Abraham saw Him in figure on Moriah. Moses saw Him at Horeb. He was an Israelite, of the house of David through Mary. He is most certainly the true Messiah. If now, I was not awakened, I was alarmed.

As I walked homeward slowly and sadly, I was startled by somebody merrily shouting near me, in long and deliberate annunciation, "Sh-o-l-u-m A-l-i-c-h-e-m." It was my brother! "Where the d— have you been? Why didn't you come home to breakfast?" I don't want breakfast, nor dinner either, I replied curtly. On hearing this, he burst out into a fit of laughter. "I suppose," taunted he, "that you have lost your 'five hundred pounds:' now it's my turn to laugh." His jocose retort excited a suspicion that I had been detected at the church. I looked him full in the face, and reading ignorance of the facts, I pushed on for home. On arriving, I was beset on all hands and made to submit to a rigid cross-examination. I told my *story* with jovial mien. Each successive falsehood looked so like truth, that they swallowed the amalgam, and then permitted me to retire to my quiet musings. I was so glad when night came, because then I retired to my solitary lodging at the warehouse. The Omniscient only knows how many severe, torturing pangs of mind I suffered. That day's experience threw down my prop. The tables were turned upon myself.

"Seek ye the Lord while He may be found, call ye upon Him while He is near. Let the wicked forsake his way and the unrighteous man his thoughts; and let him return unto the Lord, and He will have mercy upon him; and to our God, for He will abundantly pardon. For My thoughts are not your thoughts, neither are your ways My ways, saith the Lord; for as the heavens are higher than the earth, so are My ways higher than your ways, and My thoughts than your thoughts. For as the rain cometh down and the snow from heaven, and returneth not thither, but watereth the earth and maketh it bring forth and bud, that it may give seed to the sower and bread to the eater, so shall My Word be that goeth forth out of My mouth; it shall not return unto Me void, but it shall accomplish that which I please, and it shall prosper in the thing whereto I sent it." (Isaiah lv: 6-11.)

Ignorant as I then was of the practical force of this genuine *old* scripture, I could not unravel the mystery of *my first visit* to a Christian church. Similar leadings of the divine mind were, with this, made apparent in my future experience. I have with holy awe repeatedly witnessed that what the prophet says of the Lord's ways, words and thoughts, is as truthful to-day, in the preaching of Jesus Christ, as it was twenty-six hundred years ago. Perhaps the reader can remember how angry he may have been at his minister for making his condition public. You said that he literally personated you. Or perhaps you may remember how wonderful it seemed, when a sermon was preached on the identical text, subject, or theme, that had been to you a source of great perplexity. And again, how often have you left the house of God rejoicing in the great encouragement to persevere as a follower of Christ, that you received from his lips. Surely you are not ignorant, dear reader, that all of this is of the Lord. I am a believer in *special* providences. You must be also, because you are a recipient of these divine attentions as well as myself.

The Lord inspires His ministers with strong desire to preach; often He directs His servant's mind to the portion, subject, or thought best fitted to be treated, at the very time when you are inwardly prompted to break through every barrier and go to church. As a result, it may be that you continue to this day rejoicing in Christ Jesus, as by the grace of God I do now.

Never before had I realized my ignorance as I did on that day at church. And although my force was routed and myself wounded, yet, such was my inveterate hatred of Christianity, I determined to fight it to the bitter end. In vain tried I to make out that day's business nothing but a hoax, played off at my expense. Foiled on every hand, my heart grew harder. At length, reason appeared to awake; but she led me only deeper into the difficulty. I could not be reconciled to receive Christ as the Messiah, and was still determined to frustrate Christianity by means of its own words. I dared not admit even the merest probability in His favor. This much would lead me trembling into the condition of the eternally damned. Every evil power was invoked to help me. Every argument was carefully reviewed and mapped out. In my distress, they nevertheless failed me. Driven to distraction, I cried wilfully, Christ is not the Messiah; He must not be; He shall not, He shall not be.

A tedious night of troublesome dreams was at last succeeded by another morning sun, rising indeed upon "the just and the unjust." For who can fathom the deep pit of black ingratitude. Awake,

I saw that glorious luminary rapidly rising, only to
curse it; and seizing its precious light, now shining
upon the already opened testament, I used it to help
me find the internal offensive argument I was
prompted to look for.   Evil as my motive was in
reading on that occasion, yet did the Lord overrule
my work for good.   He had numbered the links in
the Devil's chain, and throughout my tribulation he
said to the enemy, " Thus far shalt thou come and
no farther."   All glory be to His holy name.

During an experience of thirty-four years in the
Christian life, I have ever noticed how much easier
it is for a man to cavil than to meet a question honorably.   Reading one day the twenty-second of Matthew, I dwelt a while on verses twenty-three and
thirty-three inclusive.   Anybody, hooted I, could
have made up that story if he had read my man,
Moses.   Compare Deut. xxv: 5–10.   But when I
read from the forty-second verse to the end of the
chapter, I confess that I was entirely at a loss.   I
tried to smother it up in the same way, only we
would have, as accomplice, David instead of Moses.
Acquainted as I was with both of these holy men, I
only now began to inquire into the meaning of their
words.   But so eager was I to find some counter
argument, that I flew in my own face, questioning
the common-sense veracity of my own acknowledged
scriptures.   The questions in the forty-second verse
appeared to be put to me, and answer them I must:
" What think ye of Christ?   Whose son is He?
They say unto him, ' The son of David.' "   The remaining verses were a perfect blank.   I could not

comprehend them. I turned to Psalm cx: 1; but all was as blank as ever. In this dilemma, I resorted to the last subterfuge of the skeptic, a very plausible reason, only predicated upon *false* premises. Can a man be the son of two men, can he have two fathers? How then can Christ be both David's son and God's son? Here two apparent arguments presented themselves, at which my wicked soul exulted. The first was the impossibility of the relationship between Christ and David. Second, reason averred that it is impossible for God, who is no corporeality, to have a son. At this, I fell back upon my old, hackneyed quibbling, if God can have one son, why not two, and why not have daughters as well? All this apeared to be too preposterous to apply to the great God. I pushed away the book, exultantly triumphant. If you ask *me* whose son you are, was my conceit, I tell you plainly in reply, either you are no son at all, or you are the son of the Devil.

Enraptured at my ingenuity in bringing such hidden mysteries to light, I concluded that I had accomplished my purpose, having produced incontrovertible arguments. Once more I smiled complacently with a settled mind. And to secure *lasting* quiet from this perplexing question, I invoked two hiding places, in one of which I thrust the book, while into the other I made crawl Moses himself.

But what can mortal man expect to accomplish when he entereth the battle against the Almighty? Let the word of the Lord give answer. "The wicked man travaileth with pain all his days, and the number of years that are laid up for the oppressor.

A dreadful sound is in his ears; in prosperity the destroyer shall come upon him. He believeth not that he shall return out of darkness, and he is destined for the sword. He wandereth abroad for bread; where is it? He knoweth that a day of darkness is ready at his hand. Trouble and anguish make him afraid—prevail against him as a king ready for the battle. For he stretcheth out his hand against God, and strengtheneth himself against the Almighty. He runneth upon him with stiffened neck, with the thick bosses of his bucklers." (Job xv: 20–26.)

This then, O mortal, is the mirror reflecting you as well as me. O, do not turn away from reproof. Alas that I did. "Hast thou an arm like God? or canst thou thunder with a voice like Him?" Yet once more listen to that voice. "The wicked are like the troubled sea when it cannot rest, whose waters cast up mire and dirt. There is *no* peace, saith my God, to the wicked." (Isaiah lvii: 20, 21.)

In spite of my determination to dismiss the entire question, I soon found that I could not quiet my conscience as easily as I had imagined. "His blood" —that last Sunday—the evidence that Messiah had been on earth, with a score of facts that appeared favorable to Christianity, crowding, pressing, and looming up before me, were a source of constant trouble, overpowering all my effort to keep calm: so much so that, as the week was passing, my desire increased to hear that same preacher and in his own church. Toward the end of the week, the impulse was irresistible. When the next Sunday arrived, I

THE BATTLE RAGING. 155

took my breakfast at home, then sauntered out for a stroll, and ere I was aware, I was on my way to "Spencer Place Chapel."

On reaching the place, I found that the congregation was gathering, so fearing that I might be detected or recognized by the preacher, I entered at another door and took my seat boldly in the body of the house. In the singing and praying I took no interest: I wanted instruction. The Lord arranged everything to meet my case; the text for the occasion was Matthew twenty-second chapter, part of the forty-second verse. "What think ye of Christ?"

His text announced, I caught a glimpse of the speaker's eye, trying as I was to detect, if possible, that design was aboard. My heart jumped; it beat hard. I looked about, and even turned around to see whether I could not leave the house; but a sense of self-respect deterred me from making so ridiculous an appearance or rather disappearance from among that large congregation. Thus, obliged to remain, I could but hear the sermon entire. The minister first stated the question explicitly. Then he proceeded to show what different people do think of Christ. Jews think that He is an impostor. The Unitarians deem Him a good man. The sinner thinks that He is unmerciful. The Christian feels that He is the Eternal God, the true Messiah. Turning from current opinions, he told us what, as he thought, we ought to think of Christ: and lastly, some of the evidences of His being all that He said He was.

I sat motionless, listening to the "man of God"

as he discoursed on the "miraculous conception in a virgin," setting forth the union of the Godhead with humanity. Christ was, on earth, "God in man." Advancing as he was victoriously with his theme, tracing "the evidences" of the Messiahship of Christ, I listened with undivided attention. Hitherto I had been motionless, unconscious of the effect of all this. Suddenly I was seized with trembling, my knees smote together. The force of Gospel truth was too keen for me. It cut down deep into my soul. I could not longer resist the conviction that *Jesus Christ* is the true Messiah. Startled from this deep thought, however, I found the enemy of my soul suggesting, "Ah, that's all very fine talk, but he has not proved that Christ is both David's and God's son." Certainly he had said enough to satisfy honest inquiry. And his time had expired. So closing his book, he announced his intention of pursuing the same subject on the next Sunday, when he would trace Christ's genealogy from Adam up, and so prove that he sprang from the tribe of Judah. At this instant it would have required considerable presence of mind to have persuaded me that all eyes were not upon me. Agitated and trembling, I looked about me for evidence that I was scrutinized. My sight failed; I could not see a single feature; all was expressionless.

When we were dismissed, I turned toward home, contemplating the mysteries of the day. So wonderful did the chain of events appear, that I would frequently exclaim, Is *this* Christianity? There were several circumstances that appeared to me to be unaccountable. But above all was the coincidence, the preacher arriving at my identical thoughts and expressing them publicly. The controversy between Jews and Christians was exhibited in so clear a light, that I felt confident he both recognized me and knew my state of mind. Upon one occasion when he became warmly engaged, he raised both his arms high, and in a loud tone of voice cried, " I would to God that there might be a Jew in this house now, listening to me." I turned pale. As he lowered his hands gradually, seeming to point them steadily toward me until they rested upon the desk—I know not why; yes I do—guilt made me dodge. " There now," chimed in Satan, " you are detected. See the treachery of this new religion. It is not half so pure as old Moses."

A very slow walk brought me home. I assumed as cheerful a countenance as possible, and artfully evaded the troublesome questions of the family. Soon I was left alone, to reflect!

O, that I could have then cheerfully yielded, I should have been spared the agonizing reflections that tormented me the whole of the week. How many times I murmured, Can it be that Christians are right after all? Is it possible that what I have heard is true? If it be true, then Jesus of Nazarath is indeed the true Messiah, while I and my father's house are lost forever. I shuddered at the thought, and in stubborn agony of soul gave vent to my feelings. No! he is not, he is not. The Christians are deluded. Christ is an impostor.—Then I would examine the evidences in His favor, not one of which could I resist.   The minister had told me that "no man has ever answered to the character which the sacred prophets give of the Saviour but Jesus of Nazareth: he has answered every particular."   I knew that what he said was true of many Jewish pretenders.   I knew that they all are proven to be nothing but base impostors.   But when I considered the perpetuity of the Christian religion; when led to observe the striking, living evidence of the Messiahship of Jesus, in the extension and effects of His religion, in bewilderment I groaned, "O God, is it true?"   If it be, then certainly "His blood" will rest angrily and forever upon us poor Jews.   He will drive us forth, to eke out a miserable existence throughout time, and afterward cast us into everlasting curses.

Hemmed in on every side by the power of God, my unyielding heart resolved to make one more desperate effort.   Never will I confess myself to be conquered, until the very last effort that I can make shall either fail me or be crushed out.   If I must fall, all my force shall fall with me!   Thus I grew desperate.   Only one, little consolation seemed now to afford me a refuge.   This was founded in the hope, aye, exultant expectation, that on the next Sunday the minister would fail to prove that Jesus Christ was both David's and God's son.   I flattered myself that I should gain this consolation, on the ground of my own reasoning.   Christians, ran my argument, cannot make it appear that they believe in but *one* God, when they try to make out three persons who, without doubt, must be three separate

Gods. All this looked so plausible that my mind became in a measure tranquil. I once more settled down quietly, scheming to carry out plans which should enable me to hear the remainder of that sermon on the following Sunday; for then I anticipated a perfect failure. *My* plan was to keep quiet. God's plan was to make it self-evident that "there is no peace to the wicked." If ever wretched man strove against the operations of the Eternal Spirit, I did during that week. I tried to close up the vision, stop the controversy, drink wine, be quiet and sleep. But the Lord said, "Not so." In spite of myself, my trouble of mind increased daily. Agony followed agony, until I wished that I could die. To this day, I am praising God for the sore trial of mind I endured that week. I was wicked; I could not have peace. A thousand times I wished that I could be reconciled to Taylor's infidelity. But no, there is a God, and a Judgment, and an Eternity to come. Thither I am hastening; and with the awful judgment in view, I trembled at the thought of meeting there none other than the hated Nazarene, if indeed He is the Saviour. Thus my moments harassed me as the time rolled on. And ere I was prepared for the dawn of the greatest day of my life so far, Sunday arrived again. I did not welcome the day. I actually trembled at the thought of going again to a Christian church. But go I must, and go I did.

At the time of starting, a mountain of temptations were thrown in my way, as obstacles against going. But I felt that I was under an obligation to hear that sermon.   So commanding all my resolution to evade the curiosity of the family, I was presently once more on the road to church.   This time I entered with the audience, as though I were one of them.   But, scarcely seated, a feeling of indescribably solemn awe crept over me.   I had never experienced anything like it in all my synagogue worship in days past.   The place was holy: I was in the presence of God!—The opening exercises were as usual. The twenty-second chapter of Matthew was read, and the text marked off was from verse forty-two to the end of the chapter.

The introduction was peculiarly impressive.   The minister now showed us *who* Christ is by treating briefly His genealogy, thus showing how he was connected with David's family.   Then came the miraculous conception in fulfilment of Isaiah vii: 14, and xi to the end, a part of which is yet to be fulfilled.   Then he spoke of the adaptedness of Jesus Christ to the necessities of mankind.   For a long time he continued to pour truth upon truth, all savoring of Christ, whom he extolled in the highest terms.   He rolled forth such volumes of Christianity that he made me see how, through this self-same, despised Jesus of Nazareth, "Heaven and earth are reconciled."   The feet of His humanity walked with us.   The hands of His divinity laid hold on the eternal Throne.   He formed a new communication for mankind from earth to glory.   To Him was to be applied the whole of Isaiah liii, and very much more.

All this I bore, though with considerable emotion. But when he spoke of the loving heart of the ever merciful Saviour, as exemplified in His praying for His enemies, "Father, forgive them for they know not what they do," thereby giving us the assurance that His very destroyers themselves might find in Him favor and pardon—ah, then I could bear up no longer. This was indeed " good *news*." I had not expected it. I had only thought of damnation. Now I am told that I, His destroyer, I, who had been all my life sanctioning the bloody deed of my fathers ; I, who had been so long fighting against Him, may, after all ! find mercy and pardon. And will He indeed pardon such a vile enemy as I? The man of God said, He will ; the word of God said, He will. Now trust Him, try Him, " come with us."

Really, this was more than I could bear. My heart beat hard ; my very soul rose to my eyes, and gushed out in a copious flood of tears. O that I could have wept on bitterly, very bitterly ; I would not have restrained a single tear. I buried my face until they sang the closing hymn. For a moment I felt a fear of detection ; and, to be sure, on venturing to raise my head that I might cautiously look around me, there, to my utter amazement, sat both M. herself and her identical mother, looking directly at me. I shrunk from their gaze, and would have sunk into the earth, if I could. Now, it flashed upon me, I'm most certainly detected ; my ruin is sealed. O how wretchedly I felt. I left the place with a crowded, bursting mind. Christ was all my thought. The Nazarene had conquered me, but I could not acknowledge myself to be beaten. When I reached my room, I silently brooded over my strange experience. Every argument but too plainly declared that Christ is truly the Messiah, the Son of God anointed.

With such reflections as these, I naturally became more despondent about the salvation of my soul. The truth that Jesus Christ was equal to His pretensions, that He is the true Messiah, God in man, the Seed of the Woman, the Shiloh, the Saviour, crowded upon me with irresistible power. So forcibly did it grapple with my mind, that often I cried out in agony, O wretched sinner that I am, how *can* I be saved? True, I had both read and heard that the worst of sinners might find pardon in Jesus; still my constant concern was, will He save most miserable me, save me from my own just deserts? *Can* I be saved? Satan would have it, "No, no! your overthrow is just." Ah, me! there is *no* hope. I must be DAMNED!

My situation appeared to be so utterly hopeless that it drove me to the brink of distraction. In my heart I cursed the rabbins because they had misled me and kept me so long in darkness. Still, I could not yield myself to Christ as my Saviour. Many days passed, leaving and finding me as changeable, as unchanged as the wind. Sometimes I was almost persuaded; then again, doubting; then yielding to an abstact probability; until I was borne on again to the fearful conclusion, He is not, He's *not;* I cannot, I *can't!*

CHAPTER XV.

MESSIAH'S VICTORY.

' Who shall lay anything to the charge of God's elect? It is God that justifieth. Who is he that condemneth? It is Christ that died, yea rather that is risen again, who is even at the right hand of God, who also maketh intercession for us. Who shall separate us from the love of Christ? shall tribulation, or distress, or persecution, or famine, or nakedness, or peril, or sword (as it is written, for thy sake we are killed all the day long, we are accounted as sheep for the slaughter)? Nay, in all these things we are more than conquerors through Him that loved us: for I am persuaded that neither death, nor life, nor angels, nor principalities, nor powers, nor things present, nor things to come, nor height, nor depth, nor any other creature shall be able to separate us from the love of God, which is in Christ Jesus, our Lord.

Subsequent experience has confirmed me in the belief of the above precious truth. But I had to learn first how unwillingly the enemy of man yields to the conquering authority of the Almighty. The · weapon that he raises against the people of God turns completely over, falling upon his own head. To-day I live a witness to this truth.

Driven to desperation, I resolved upon one more effort to destroy Christianity with its own weapons. To accomplish this, I proposed to read the New Testament regularly through. This time I determined to make an honest business of it. So with the Old Testament on one side, the New on the other, and the Hebrew in front of me, I formally commenced, comparing one with the other as I progressed.

"Now I'll end the controversy." The more laborious my research, the more was I impressed with the true character of Jesus. If I had been acquainted with the New Testament when an infidel, I should have said with Porphyry that it was all written "after the events." In the person of Jesus Christ I found an exact fulfilment of the old prophecies. I was struck with the harmony between the two books throughout. *Existing* facts attested their common truth. My own nation were wide-spread witnesses. If Daniel and Isaiah had lived at the time of Christ, there might be some ground to suspect a forgery. But from their respective periods of about five and seven hundred years before the nativity of Jesus, both speak so accurately respecting the time of His birth, His character, life, passion, death, and resurrection, that I could no longer permit a particle of doubt to remain with me. By the time I had finished the New Testament, I cried out, "Depart from me, O Lord, for I am a sinful man."

The examination of the sacred books occupied several weeks, each day of which passed leaving me still stronger in the faith of Christ. By this time I perfectly knew what would be the temporal consequence of receiving Christ as my Saviour. I did not feel strong enough for the ordeal that I knew must necessarily be undergone. In my very self had been disclosed evidence that the same inveterate spirit which characterized my people when they madly "cried out the more exceedingly, crucify Him," and when "answered all the people and said, His blood be on us and on our children," clung to them maliciously as ever. The word of Christ admonished me to "count the cost." I saw the truth, I read the truth, and in my heart I felt its power. I had no more opposition arguments; and consequently yielded to the only alternative, by force of circumstances, to receive Christ as the only true Messiah, and give credit to all His pretensions. Well, what now? I believe! Am I therefore secure? In vain the enemy replied, yes. Another Spirit within me was swift in finding a different verdict. No, you are ignorant of true repentance; you are not a Christian yet. And well did I know that I was very far from being a Christian. When I sat hearing the man of God discourse about the mercy of Jesus, it afforded me at the time great consolation. But now that I just began to see my own character, the more I contemplated that mercy the more ocean-like in magnitude did my sins spread out; and staring defiantly at me, they each frowningly asked,-Dare *you* expect mercy from Him? Too ready, alas, was I to yield to the wicked one, and in despair to echo, There is no mercy for me; the Christian religion is true, and I am lost.

This state of mind continued many days. My health seemed to be exhausted. Nothing that the family physician could prescribe reached my case. He said that my mind was affected, and that I would soon pass off in a decline. I alone knew that I needed the Heavenly Physician. Every leisure hour that I could secure in private was devoted to acquiring religious knowledge. I soon learned, therefore, some of the high moral duties that grow out of my new religion. Consequently I began to think kindly of those good Christians whom I had persecuted, and was disposed to make, if possible, reparation no less than confession. There, for instance, was that young lady M——, how, I wondered, can I ever see her again? Never have I appeared so despicably mean in my own eyes as at this time while thinking about her. I wanted so much to tell her about Jesus, but I dare not visit her again. Then there was, under my own roof, the faithful boy, Thomas; a sketch of whose history I expect to add in an appendex. Him, however, I resolved to invite to lodge with me again at the warehouse, and at a convenient opportunity disburden my mind to him. He came; a long time succeeded, but I was tongue-tied no less on his arrival than later. He must have noticed a change in my conduct generally, but especially towards him. Still I dreaded the consequences of a disclosure. I could not suffer for Christ's cause. I still read my testament privately, though I did not dare to say a single word to anybody.

In consequence of my weakness, several days rolled on in irresolution, which kept me trembling under the ire of a justly-incensed Deity. My sinful life, a blasphemed God, a crucified Saviour, an insulted Spirit, Death, Judgment, Eternity, with the condition of the saved and that of the lost—these all were continually before me. My sins therefore rising like a mountain, threatened to crush me. Many a time in my agony I raved out, What shall I do to be saved? I cannot live; I cannot die; I cannot, O how can I meet Jesus at the judgment day! Would that

I had nothing to do! O that there was indeed no God!

Not yet had I learned the great theme of " salvation by grace." The religion of my former life was one of unceasing work. Now I had to learn how rather to trust the Messiah. I did not know what this thing, Faith, could mean. Prayers I had often read, but never had I yet prayed. I was soon, however, to see the initiatory of my Christian pilgrimage.

CHAPTER XVI.

CAPTIVE EXILE LOOSED.

One evening the boy Thomas asked leave of absence for the night. Once more I am alone in that little back-room of a large five-story building. It was sufficiently solitary to awaken the gloomiest thoughts of the severe ordeal awaiting me. Meditating upon the Christian religion and my prospect of salvation, I felt something to be yet wanting—something, I did not know what. I believed that Christ was the very Messiah; but the idea that He was *my* Messiah, this I did not grasp. How to arrive personally at this elevated consciousness I did not know. I thought of death with dread. I anticipated my just deserts after death, and in terror wailed, *must* I then be damned? Is there *no* hope for me? Is there no *possible* chance for escape? Must I be lost in my ignorance? Is there no man who will teach me? My rabbins are blind; my brethren are in darkness; my associates cannot help me. Father will kill me, or with the whole family, thrust me contemptuously away. Christians I know can and would help me. M. is willing to teach me. But then I dare not communicate my feelings to anybody. I feared the Jews. My life, if diverted from its wonted channel, would be in danger. I shuddered at this because I dreaded death. I knew too well that I was not ready for Eternity!

I paced my room in trouble, crying out, what shall I do? What shall I do? I'm lost! Thus in despair I sat down to my table, lighted a candle, and opened my well read Testament. The portion open before me was the sixth of Matthew. Every single letter of it imparted a volume of instruction. I read the whole chapter with deep and pungent emotion. It reached my heart; I felt its power. It riveted itself to me. I also was riveted to it; I had no desire to read any further. My whole soul was fastened upon that one chapter. A new thought aroused me: you have never prayed—try the effect of prayer! I was startled, for the thought seemed new. Never had I dreamed of such a remedy. Pray! How shall I pray? I'm not a Christian. Here I seemed more intelligently to inquire, what must I do? Pray as the Christians do, came the response. What, questioned I, must I actually go down on my knees to pray? My proud heart recoiled at the idea. The Testament being still open at the same place, I read again the form of prayer given by Jesus and commencing at the ninth verse. My monition was, Say that on your knees. I trembled with fear, and trembling I kneeled down. I began to say, Our Father who art in heaven, hallowed . . . . Here my physical powers left me. My mind was dreadfully alarmed. I thought that somebody was in my room toward whom I entertained great dread. On my knees, trembling like a leaf, the earth seemed now to open beneath me. I could see the flames of hell vainly shooting up to reach me. "Stop," expostulated Satan, "consider what you are doing; remember how great your sin is. First, you are going to violate the command of Jehovah, 'Honor thy father and thy mother;' consequently you will soon die, your days will be cut off from the earth while you are yet young, and your soul will be with me forever. Second, you are going to turn Christian. By that act you will be forsaking your father's God, to worship a stranger, Jesus the crucified one—and for that sin, if alone, you must be damned forever. Arise from your knees and be at peace as you are."

In an instant I was on my feet. Confusedly I looked about my room. I saw no disarrangement: there were my chair, the table and the open Testament, just as I left them. I did not seem to realize my condition; so throwing myself in the chair, I leaned back in bewilderment. What does all this mean? As if audibly, the answer returns, Pray. I have tried to do so, but cannot. Still the response insisted, Pray. But, how shall I pray? *Pray*, PRAY, PRAY, was still oracularly repeated. And still I murmured, I know not how to pray; I can't pray! In a few minutes a new thought occurred to me, I had not prayed aright; I must follow the rule exactly. Once again I referred to the book. I read the fifth verse in alarm. That is truth, I confessed. But I have done with all that: what next? Read on! "But thou, when thou prayest, enter into thy closet, and when thou hast shut thy door, pray to thy Father which is in secret: and thy Father

which seeth in secret shall reward thee openly."
Here then was my rule. First, enter the closet.
Well, here I am all alone. Second, shut the door.
It was shut, but not locked; so I locked it. Third,
pray to thy Father. Here I paused, thinking of this
wonderful Jesus. He tells me to pray to the *Father*,
not himself—the Father Almighty, Jehovah of the
Jews. Well, what next? I could not learn that
here. So looking over the entire field of operation
and supposing that I could strengthen secrecy, I
drew my bedstead up to the locked door. Now I
was ready. Lighting a fresh candle, I sat down to
meditate. In an instant my mental tribulation increased with ten-fold fury. My soul was wrought
up to the highest excitement by the temptations of
the devil, the voice of the Lord, and the dictates
of my own conscience. At length I resolved to try
to pray by rule. So I went down on my knees to
repeat the same words. But I had scarcely begun
to speak, ere I commenced struggling. The devil
tempted me maliciously. My whole soul, however,
was wrought upon by a stronger power, constraining
me to pray. Spiritually I seemed to be on fire; my
power of speech was taken from me. On my knees
I bent, agonizing before God with tears and groans.
After some time my tongue was released, my speech
returned. In an instant I cried out, O Lord, God
of my fathers, Abraham, Isaac and Jacob! Hear
me, O God! What is truth? If Moses be true,
give me Moses: if Christ be true, give me Christ.
I could not say another word. Broken down at the
foot of the cross, I could advance nothing more than

idle tears. I expected to receive in some way an answer. Was this faith? The "vision tarried," but I waited for it, waited on my knees. It came: I knew all about it in an instant. There before my face, at a comfortable distance, appeared a large cross, and Jesus was stretched upon it. I looked at Him without fear. My Lord, I cried. He did not speak, but smiled upon me so, that angels' tongues cannot describe the scene. All my doubts vanished. The Holy Spirit took me and pointed to the words above the cross, "I am the truth." So the vision departed. My soul leaped within me. Every scriptural assurance of pardon and acceptance brightened up, and beamed full with its lustre upon me. Now I know that all, all my sins are pardoned. The scriptures of God were opened wide to my understanding, so that I received joyfully all the promises.

I now thought of Death, Judgment and Eternity without the least terror. Every feeling of fear was gone. I could have willingly died at that time. But I did not ask nor wish for death. Life began to look glorious. I felt like a pardoned criminal, and gave full liberty to my soul in shouting, Glory, glory, glory to the Lord! I'm free, I'm free, I continued, and as if becoming physically free, rose to my feet. My candle was burned quite down; but the whole gloomy building appeared illuminated. My soul magnified the Lord: I felt as though I should never experience another pang.

'Twas a heaven below
My Redeemer to know,
And the angels could do nothing more
Than to fall at His feet,
And the story repeat,
And the Saviour of sinners adore.

Walking about my room in ecstacy, I shouted, I'm free, I'm free: glory, glory to God, I'm free. I clasped my Testament and bathed it with joyful tears, kissing the precious book, and extolling the beautiful religion that teaches me to adore the Lamb of God. Now I could think of "His blood" with a sensation of mingled joy and grief. The horrible spell was broken; Jesus broke it. The curse was removed: the devil was conquered; and my poor soul set at liberty. Bless Jehovah, O my soul, and all that is within me bless His holy name. Thanks to God who giveth *me* the victory through *my* Lord Jesus Christ.

And now, if I did not firmly believe that in " a dream, a vision of the night," the Lord showed me what I should be called upon to endure for Christ's sake, I would not introduce what follows. I cannot apologize for what I write because I write the truth. But I can bend a little familiarly toward the reader. You do not believe in " visions." Well, certainly I cannot compel faith. It must remain for you to prove to the world that under *no circumstances* whatever does the Lord make known His will to His people now as in days of old. But you will say, the Bible is sufficient revelation for us. So it is, when it meets all the purposes for which it is intended. But *suppose* it should be the Lord's will that you must go to the Arctic regions and make disciples of a newly discovered people. How will you find it out? Will you look in the Bible for *your* call under these circumstances? I know the religion of our blessed Saviour deals liberally in calls for laborers to work in His vineyard, both in a general way and everywhere. But *you* are wanted for that particular locality. How, I ask, will the mind of the Lord be made clearly known to you? You confess to having a strong desire to isolate yourself from your loving associations of home for the spiritual benefit of the Arctic regions. This irrepressible conflict is a new revelation to you, whether your *first* impression occurred in the day-time or night. A *true* vision *is* a revelation. Caution is needed here; but visions must not altogether be denied.

Being in a state of utter exhaustion, I threw myself upon the bed, but as will be readily understood, I could not sleep. About midnight, I thought that I was walking out. The air was balmy, all was serene, even the sky having doffed every vestige of cloud. Quickly there gathered above my head, a cloud, the very blackest I ever saw. I stood a while gazing at it, wondering what it meant. Suddenly from its immediate centre burst through a most brilliant orb, round as the moon, bright as the sun. I noticed that it shot its rays nowhere but upon me. They were exquisitely bright; yet standing fully in front of it, my eye could endure its steady blaze without the least blinking. In a moment I was filled with ecstacy, and enraptured, cried out, what is it Lord? I heard a voice that answered, Light out of darkness. O Lord, I asked, is it I? Yes, was the reply, and the vision disappeared.

A sense of sweet tranquility possessed my mind. I realized that I was in the presence of the Lord. At that hour it would have been utterly impossible for any evil spirit to have alarmed me, so sacredly tranquil was my whole soul. Yet the terrible enemy that had held me prisoner so, alas, so long, could not suffer me to escape from him without making a strong effort to counteract the effects that the "vision of the Almighty" had had upon me.

My tranquil season therefore must be broken up. In a short time, probably within an hour, my room was instantly filled with huge, venomous reptiles of every description. One of monstrous proportions acted as chief. I shrunk from them in terror. They seemed to take advantage of my alarm, and with a hellish exultation (which raised my hair and shook my frame) they formed themselves into a long double row facing each other. There they stood side by side, most maddened, hideous serpents. Their awful chief was stationed at the head. Down upon me gazed all their terrible eyes. Presently the chief commanded me to take up that gauntlet. My fear was very great; perspiration dropped from upon me. I commenced to approach the old serpent, when suddenly he darted his horrible fangs at me, his eyes standing out, burning balls full of malice. I trembled, but took one step more. Satan, for he it was that proved to be the chief, made a desperate effort to grasp me; but as I noticed, some mysterious power held him back. "Fear not, I am with thee," came forcibly into my mind. I began to take a little courage, and stepped into the line of fiends. Every one of those dreadful serpents attempted in turn to entangle me in his slimy and complicated folds. They also were restrained: they were utterly unable to harm me. When I saw this I grew really bold: my fear left me, and I folded my arms with a sense of security, for faith came to help me. On, on, on I walked in the passage way between them. Every step increased their rage, and no less my courage. At last I arrived at the end. There stood my father. Father, I exclaimed, and would have run to him for protection. But I noticed that he looked at me with exceeding anger, and having a club in his uplifted hand, threatened to crush me as soon as I neared him. But he too was restrained from hurting me. I am through, safely through. In surprise I stood awhile, looking at him steadily and fearlessly; then this vision vanished like its predecessor.

The hours till sunrise passed in very serious reflections upon what I had experienced. I had no difficulty in making a personal application of all three visions. The one at the evening prayer spoke for itself. Jesus, the one Messiah and my own Lord, had died for me. I am saved in consequence. Then it is manifested that I am "light out of darkness." Hereafter, therefore, I must separate myself from my former darkness. Had I been better grounded in biblical truth, I should have inferred my duty from Matthew v: 29, 30, but what I lacked in knowledge the Lord showed me in vision.

The next dream I understood as pointing me to my future walk in the Christian course. The Lord forewarned and forearmed me for a terrible conflict. I must suffer tribulation; I must pass through the midst of malignant enemies. My dear father himself would be my bitterest foe. I should, however, be almost miraculously preserved and sustained. Therefore I must be strong, and in faith go forward. Testimony to the truth of the Lord in Jesus Christ must be borne before many enemies, who thereupon would vent their rage, but all in vain.

I regarded myself now as "born again:" I had become a new creature in Jesus the Messiah. Many years have passed since that eventful night. Never, for a single moment, have I forgotten or even slighted that heavenly admonition. The belief that God makes special revelations for special purposes, to His chosen servants, strengthens with my years. How much all this had to do with my future life and destiny, shall duly appear.

12

CHAPTER XVII.

THE NEWS PROCLAIMED.

"When He was come nigh, even now at the descent of the mount of Olives, the whole multitude of the disciples began to rejoice and praise God with a loud voice for all the mighty works that they had seen; saying, Blessed be the King that cometh in the name of the Lord: Peace in Heaven and glory in the highest. And some of the Pharisees . . . . said unto Him, Master, rebuke Thy disciples. But He answered and said unto them, I tell you if these should hold their peace, the stones would immediately cry out."

In overwhelming sorrow or overflowing joy, O for a friend, a true friend, to whom we can speak. Let us give full liberty to the audible voice of anguish, and not try to suppress it, or the result may be a lamentable confusion of mind. A wiser than Solomon taught this philosophy, when He applied it to His rejoicing disciples. They *must* cry out, they must sing, they must shout. Their physical and moral good demands full liberty, the soul's rightful freedom.

I had passed through so much mental anguish that now my joy knows no bounds. I did not know any spiritual song of the Christians, but my heart was full of singing; so the reader may apply to my case a stanza which he may have often sung:

> Now methinks I hear him praising,
> Publishing to all around,
> Friends, is not my case amazing:
> What a Saviour I have found.

The blessed morning dawned and introduced fresh joys, aye, joys entirely new. Never had I imagined it possible for the atmosphere of London to be fragrant. But on this holy morning it was so, at least to me. The sun shone beautifully—a rare occurrence in that misty horizon. Every object about me appeared to be charming. Never before had I seen the beauty of the Lord shine so resplendently as on that sacred morning. The all-glorious I Am, the ever blessed Jesus had taken up His residence in my heart. The Devil was vanquished, and ceased to annoy me. O, how I loved the Lord. My soul doth magnify the Lord, and my spirit hath rejoiced in God my Saviour. This I could truly echo.

Now I must speak out, I must *tell* somebody, or my heart will burst with emotion. I must go out into the open streets and proclaim Jesus. I thought no more of *consequences*. Speak I must. God, help me. He will, He does; for just at this juncture the bell rings. I start; is it timidity? I pause. The bell rings again. At this I rouse up and run below to open the door. In a moment I am filled with laughing. I open the door. Thomas, the faithful, has come much too early to open the house, although he was always first on hand. My heart beat: a thousand thoughts rushed through my mind rapidly. What course shall I pursue—shall I make known to him at once the glad tidings, or watch for a convenient opportunity? But I was too happy to deliberate. I opened the door, laughing. He came in, and looked at me very suspiciously. " Good mornin', zur; you appear very pleasant this mornin', zur."

My heart swelled to bursting, and I turned away. I
could hold out no longer, and determined at once to
unbosom all my heart to him. I did not know how
to begin, but going up to him I threw my arms
around him in embrace. In a moment the strong
youth had shaken me off and broken loose from me.
Then he began to reprove me for my conduct, supposing that I had been out all night reveling, and
that I was now intoxicated. "You're too foolish,
zur. Let me alone. If ye don't, I'll tell yer father,
zur. Stand back, zur, and let me open the shop."
I knew all about my former conduct to him (see appendex) and felt that I merited this rebuke. I could
not reply, but turning away, broke down and wept
aloud. "What's the matter, zur?" O Thomas,
can the Lord certainly forgive me!—Yes, yes, He
has forgiven me; and cannot you? Confused and
overcome he asked, "What do yer mean, zur?" I
could not tell him any more, but just said, "Jesus,"
and wept on.

He had heard enough to assure him what the
matter was: he was in possession of a secret that I
had yet to learn. He knew the Shibboleth of Zion.
He had heard from my lips two words, "Forgive,
and Jesus." In a moment he caught the idea. Literally jumping, he caught me in his arms, and wept
and laughed at the same time. I wanted those arms,
those tears, that laugh; and he wanting the same
from me, received them out of my inmost soul as we
laughed and wept, locked in each other's arms. At
last he could speak. "Now," he exclaimed, "God
has answered my prayer. When you used to perse-

cute me for Jesus' sake, you know, zur, I never re-
taliated. And do you remember, zur, when you
tried to put my head in the dog-trough?" I do.
" Well, you hurt me very much, and I went and
told my Heavenly Father of you; and I prayed the
Lord to convert you; and He's done it, zur, He's forgiven you, zur, for Christ's sake; and I forgive you
too from the very bottom of my heart, I do forgive
you; God knows I do. I tell you, zur, there's a hot
trial afore you. You're got a hard row to hoe, a
heavy persecution's ahead for you. I won't stay
here to see it, cause I can't help you; but it must
come. God will be your helper; I know He will.
His grace will be sufficient for you; and I shall leave
this place soon as possible. Now, zur, you be quiet
until the time comes; the Lord don't want you to
run your head in the fire. I know what's comin',
and you must be quiet until it comes. Pray to the
Lord, and ——. The hands are comin', I must open
the shutters."

I learned volumes from this boy during the following week. When the next Saturday night came, he
quit my father's employ without assigning any reason; and no offer of higher wages could induce him
to remain. Thus after having served my father
about seven years for weekly wages, he is content
with seeing his prayers answered in the conversion
of my poor, darkened, persecuting, Jewish soul; and
then, without having any fixed plans for the future,
he left that he might not see the persecution which
he knew must come upon me.

Never have my spirits been sunk so low as on the

Saturday night when we parted privately. O Thomas, I shall be alone; and I wept. "You will not be alone, zur; God will be with you, zur." I buried my face, weeping harder. When he turned to leave me, he grasped my hand, but could not speak another word. My heart swelled to breaking. I loved him for Messiah's sake, "sorrowing most of all for the words which he spake, that they should see his face no more."

CHAPTER XVIII.

LIGHT OUT OF DARKNESS.

"Seeing we have this ministry as we have received mercy, we faint not: but have renounced the hidden things of dishonesty, not walking in craftiness, nor handling the Word of God deceitfully; but by manifestation of the truth, commending ourselves to every man's conscience in the sight of God. But if our Gospel be hid, it is hid to them that are lost, in whom the God of this world hath blinded the minds of them which believe not, lest the light of the glorious Gospel of Christ, who is the image of God, should shine unto them. For we preach not ourselves, but Christ Jesus the Lord; and ourselves your servants for Jesus' sake. For God, who commanded the light to shine out of darkness, hath shined in our hearts, to give the light of the knowledge of the glory of God in the face of Jesus Christ."

A young convert to the religion of Jesus needs to remain very long within the walls of Zion's schoolhouse in order to learn the meaning of that teaching, "The law *was* our schoolmaster to bring us to Christ." Now, he must have done with that pedagogue and enter the rank and file of the sacred, military school. There are tactics for the student of sanctifying knowledge; and the sooner he receives his first lesson the better for him. The prophet Jonah felt quite secure when, in addition to the booth which he made, his head was sheltered from the scorching rays of the sun by a large-leafed, luxuriant gourd vine, which the Lord prepared for him. But when it seemed good in the mind of Jehovah to do what He would with His own, preparing a worm which lived upon His vine, and leaving the head of the poor prophet without shelter against the morrow's sun, lo we find him complaining bitterly; in anger, he wished that he could die. Poor Jonah! he did not know Jesus.

Thomas has left us, my gourd is dried up; O how defenceless I feel. For some time I had a feeling of desolation. Within a few days, while Thomas had yet been with me, I learned to depend upon him for counsel. Every chance I could snatch, a question would be asked of him. In fact, I depended upon him to support me. But he is gone now, and I am left to be tempted by the wicked one. " My feet were almost gone, my steps had well nigh slipped;" for I had not yet learned the danger of making "flesh my arm." This, therefore, must be my first lesson. The Lord sustained me: He received my fainting hope. He bade me rejoice again in Him, and teaching me how to bear it, sanctified affliction as I leaned upon the strong arm of Jehovah by faith in Jesus, for strength and support in all my future trials.

Hitherto I had been so entirely absorbed in my own trouble, that it is only at this time I am prepared to advance in divine life. Hourly I grow stronger, declaring, " O God, my heart is fixed." With fixedness of purpose, the Throne of Grace will bear witness how agonizingly I prayed for every member of the family by name. In a brief space of time the family circle proved a field by far too small to confine my sympathies. How I wanted to tell everybody about Jesus. Were my arms as roomy as my heart, I would lift up the world of sinners and set them down at the right hand of the throne where Jehovah Jesus sits. Nor was this by any means a mere fitful or transient disposition. No, no; it gained strength with my daily growth in gaace. Two strong evidences sustain me in this belief. The first was an awaking desire to preach the Gospel; the second, that I have preached Christ from that day to the present time. My call to the ministry was given at this early period, and, glory be to my Heavenly Father, I have since endeavored to labor in behalf of a perishing world. I love this beautiful world for Christ's sake. Life is glorious in the service of Jesus. I love my fellow man. I love you, dear readers, and " pray you in Christ's stead be ye reconciled to God."

No truth in medical science is any better founded (as proved by actual test) than that slow and lasting passions, such as hopeless love, grief, despair, etc., if suffered to usurp supremacy, will bring on chronic disease. In vain do you afterward apply medicine until the passion which caused the disease is discovered and calmed. For the accomplishment of such a humane work, the religion of Jesus Christ supplies the surest and safest remedy, the love of God. It is the sovereign cure for all mental miseries, effectually preventing all bodily disorders the passions generate, by keeping the passions themselves within due bounds, and by the unspeakable calm, serenity, and tranquility it gives the mind. Thus, if for no other reason, this remedial agent rises high as the heavens above all others.

Soon as this precious religion became my settled portion for life, my general health improved and my countenance assumed a brighter aspect than it had worn for many months past. This change was soon noticed by the family, and Dr. Kish applauded to the skies. When, however, I assured them that I had not taken the first atom of the doctor's medicine, but had thrown it all away, they were not a little perplexed in guessing what had wrought so sudden and so great a change. The time had not yet come for me to tell them. But I did want to tell somebody. I will go again to visit M., and tell her that "His blood" has availed for me. I'll tell her in tears that I am broken down at the foot of the cross. How much I wish to tell her. Yes, I can go there and——. No, no, I cannot, I dare not: such has been my conduct that she could not believe me. I will openly avow myself a Christian, then I can go.

It is needless to say that during all this time I read very little else but my Testament. I had been used to exploring books all my life, so that I had no difficulty in arriving at an understanding of the letter on Christian duty. I began, therefore, to think very seriously about being baptized into a profession of the Christian faith. I cannot say that I was entirely free from the dread of consequences; and prudence dictated to me the necessity of seeking Christian advice. My first step, therefore, was to ask counsel of God: this done, my next led me to find the minister whom I had heard preach, and tell him all my heart. Once in the neighborhood of his church, there was no difficulty in following directions to his house.

After a little longer walk, I arrived at his door with a clear conscience, but beating heart. There I halted, hesitated, deliberated, almost failed. O, my blessed Lord, help me for Christ's sake, amen. I am strong now. Never till my departure hence shall I forget the peculiar emotions of mind arising when I had actually knocked at his door, which was so quickly opened, that no time remained for procrastination.

Wonder of wonders! I am in the home of a " Jesus Christ's man." Many a time had I been in the houses of the Devil's men, and reveled and reviled there with steady nerve. But now that I am in the presence of a Christian minister, for the first time too, I tremble. The venerable man received me smilingly and with such beautiful courtesy that I was at once impressed with the idea that I was not the first pilgrim to the Holy Land who had received a hearty welcome from him. And this became apparent, as he so readily comprehended the nature of my business with him. He introduced the subject of religion, and encouraged me to tell him why I appeared so sad. His kind words distilled into my heart, and permeated through every emotion of my soul. My nerves became steady, I gathered strength, took courage, and telling him my simple story, expressed a wish to be baptized.

All the religion with which I had come into contact in former days was insufficient to produce one holy emotion. But the very first person who ventured to speak to me about Jesus from the fulness of her pure heart, *wept*. Then I read in the testament

two words, which at the first sight seemed to reproach my infidelity and check my Jewish prejudice:
Jesus wept. When my own heart broke down under the force of gospel truth, I wept. When the
faithful boy Thomas understood that God had answered his prayer in converting my darkened soul,
he clasped me in his arms, and wept. And now that
I have told my simple, broken story in the hearing
of a man of God and his sympathizing wife, they
both wept. What a truthful and wonderful religion
is this, which makes a man feel that he has a soul,
which will not let him be a stoic, but brings out
both his joys and his sorrows, indulging his smile,
but drying his tear.

The story I told evidently produced intense emotion. For some time the good man was absorbed in
deep thought. On recovering he fixed his fatherly
eyes upon me, speaking in so kind and reasonable a
manner that I felt satisfied I had found at last what
I so ardently desired, a spiritual adviser. He said,
"Mr. Davis, if your narration is true, you have much
to encounter. Christianity encourages caution; and
it is important that you should be well established in
Gospel truth before you make a public profession.
You are young, rich in this world, and move in a
respectable circle of society. If you embrace Christianity, you will have to sacrifice all that you are
worth on earth for Christ's sake. Now when you
shall have been cast out from home and affluence
upon a world of strangers and poverty, if afterward
it appears that you have been mistaken, your last
state will be worse than the first. Take, therefore,

more time; sit down and count the cost. You have
the same Bible that I have; the same God whom
I worship, you worship. Go home, my young
friend, to your father's house; remain quiet there a
little while longer. Pray to the Lord to give you
direction. Read your Testament again; *don't neglect
the Epistles.* If, when you shall have considered de-
liberately what you are about to undertake and suffer for Jesus Christ, you conclude it is your duty to
take up your cross and follow Jesus through evil
report, come back and tell me." Here he lifted up
holy hands and tearful eyes and prayed, "May the
God of Abraham, and of Isaac, and of Jacob direct
you, for Christ's sake. Amen." He then took my
right hand in both of his, and held me firmly while
he blessed me with a parting benediction. Through
the whole of this interview, I had acquitted myself
heroically, restraining every emotion, through fear I
should lose a word. But now the interview is ended,
I have received a parting blessing, the hold on my
hand is slackening, but on my heart it is fastening.
My hitherto restrained emotions absolutely refuse to
be kept under another second. While yet another
"God Almighty bless you" quivered upon the lips
of the servant of Jesus, my heart overflowed, and in
a shower of joyful, grateful tears, I left his house.

On my way home I was severely tempted by the
Devil. "Consider well what you must sacrifice for
a crucified man. Take care of your reputation.
You are just as well off as you are. You can believe
in Christ just as much, if you remain at home without being baptized. Why not then be quiet about

it? Hang on to your property anyhow! O, you fool, you will lose all you are worth if you are baptized. Can't you be a Christian without baptism?" All at once, coming in sight of home, I awaked suddenly to find that I had not been thinking at all about the words I had heard. I seemed to start up from a dream. What does this mean? this is satan's delusion! Get thee behind me, satan; Christ is my rock!

Without losing a minute, I commenced to read my Testament again. This time *I began with the Epistles*, and, ending with the Gospels, I gave it a very careful reading, calmly dwelling upon every word and doctrine. The final result was that I must be baptized into the Christian faith. I did not then know that Christians differ about baptism, but thought that of course all Christians were taught alike out of their own little book. I had heard of christening but not of baptism; and now that I want to be baptized, I do not know how it is to be done. All my readings about this act directed me to some water deep enough for a man of full size to go into it. But I was ignorant about the mode of proceeding, and in fact everything else beyond what I read of "going down into the water," "much water," "the river," "buried thereby," and thus "putting on Christ." All these incidents seemed to import but one harmonious idea about baptism. I dreamed not for a moment that I could possibly make a mistake. One thought bothered me a little, founded on Romans vi. 4: "We are buried with Him by baptism," etc. In my ignorance, of course I reasoned ignorantly. What is this *burying?* Are all Christians buried in the water? How long are they kept under? Why, if they are *buried* in water, they must drown. But they appear to be all alive, somehow. Well, well, what is safe for them, is safe for me. And what is duty for them, is duty for me. So whatever it is, sink or swim, drown or float—anything—God will take care of me, and *I will* be baptized.

My mind is now at rest. I have decided upon my future course. Hereafter another train of thought must engross my mind, resulting from the extraordinary position that I am now taking. I begin to feel the fangs of persecution. I must be an outcast. The first taste of the cup is bitter. Where shall I go after I am cast out; what shall I do to make a living? I had weighed well every word and thought, and now I am weighing action. I must unite with the Christians. I looked well to Messiah's legacy, "In the world ye shall have tribulation." But Christ had overcome the world by His patience in suffering. So I took courage, and buckled on my armor. (Eph. vi: 11.)

In solitude I read the precious little book. It seems to confirm my worst apprehensions of the result. Well, they will cast me out; I shall lose all my property. I feel now that I can endure all this for Christ's sake. But the thought of parting with my dear relatives, perhaps forever, this pierced my soul. In quiet musings a tear would ever and anon trickle, involuntarily trickle down my cheeks and fall upon my open Testament. Part with my loved relations! O my God. Faith and dread struggled within me for the ascendency. One up, and then the other, they wrestled, overthrowing and still striving, until a sentiment hard to be described, would arouse me and literally throw me down upon my knees, so that as a weaned child I heartily moaned.

It was this kind of devotion that sometimes led my soul to contemplate Messiah's love until I wished myself away from earth that I might be present with the ever-blessed Redeemer. Earth would lose its charms; my loved ones fade from mind. The Eternal Father in the glorious Messiah calling himself a son, overcame all my hesitancy by His absorbing love. By His unfailing grace, I can now follow Him at any sacrifice. Did I expect to be privately murdered for my new religion's sake? Life I could not hold dear that I might fully win and follow my gracious Saviour.

Light and darkness alternating with the return of every day or the presentation of each new duty, I was like a foe on the battle field, firmly meeting reverses because fortified by a consciousness of right in the struggle, undergoing defeat to-day, only to be more determined upon victory to-morrow, steadfast in the contest though the ranks be thinned, and looking hourly for the hotly contested struggle that must decide, by the fortune of war, the result of the present quarrel.

Just learning to fight the good fight of faith, with foes to encounter who are terribly real, I must assume the initiative, must bring on the battle. But what a wonderful contest! obliged to offend, I will be suffered to defend. I am to tell my dear, kind father that I am a Christian, and *must* suffer the consequences. At first I boasted, let them come, I will tell father the very first opportunity. My resolution, however, was not so easily carried out. I forgot that we wrestle not against flesh and blood, but against principalities, powers, the rulers of the darkness of this world, and spiritual wickedness in high places. But I am soon reminded of this, Pauline experience as well as revelation. A quiet shot from the hidden foe strikes into my weakest part. "How can you—most ungrateful, selfish wretch that you are—how can you approach your indulgent father and tell him, yes tell to him your dreadfully hateful story? How can you dare to tell him that you are a 'meshumut,' a turncoat? You will break his heart: you will bring down his gray hairs through sorrow to the grave. Then you are a murderer, and will be made to feel what it is thus to trifle with an indulgent parent." Ah, wily Satan, you have me. I confess that I hesitate. I cannot tell my dear, dear father. I do not value my life so much as his tranquility. No, I cannot tell him. I will keep my new religion to myself.

Here I must have forever rested, but for "Him that rideth upon the heavens of heavens which were of old. Lo, He doth send out His voice, a mighty voice. He that loveth father or mother more than me is not worthy of me, and he that loveth son or daughter more than me is not worthy of me: and he that taketh not his cross and followeth after me is not worthy of me." I knew it all, but I had read

13

just before that a man's foes shall be they of his own household. To all this my faithless heart responded, but I shall be an outcast, and wander about the earth, separated from all that is dear to me, and hated by those I love. The prospect was dark, yet the Lord Jehovah was light about me. " Say to them that are of a fearful heart, Be strong, fear not; behold your God will come with vengeance, even God with a recompense: He will come and will save you." (Isaiah xxxv: 4.) " Fear thou not, for I am with thee; be not dismayed, for I am thy God. I will strengthen thee, yea I will help thee, yea I will uphold thee with the right hand of my righteousness." (Isaiah xli: 10.) Something just here seemed to whisper, so lovingly, " Can you doubt your dear Saviour's protection?" No, no, I do not doubt my blessed Jesus in anything He has said. And those glorious promises, how precious they are. But father has ever remembered the dying words of my precious mother, " Take care of Jonas ;" and he has been a good, kind father to me. Besides, he is a very prominent member of the great synagogue, both on account of his wealth and because this year he occupies a conspicuous office. This brings him under the special notice of the whole of that great congregation. These considerations will add to his mortification, rendering my chance for life ten-fold more precarious. The more I looked at the situation, the darker it grew, and in all probability I should have yielded to these satanic impulses, had not the blessed Jehovah interposed again with trumpet tones, which pealed upon my soul like inspiration. "He that is for us is more than all they who are against us. Do you believe this?" Yes, Lord: and in a moment my soul took fresh courage, and turning its eyes inward became its own reprover. "Why art thou cast down, O my soul? and why art thou disquieted in me? Hope thou in God, for I shall yet praise Him for the help of His countenance."

Then "be strong in the Lord and in the power of His might. Put on the whole armor of God, that ye may be able to stand against the wiles of the devil. . . . Stand, therefore, having your loins girt about with truth, and having on the breastplate of righteousness, and your feet shod with the preparation of the gospel of peace; above all, taking the shield of faith wherewith ye shall be able to quench all the fiery darts of the wicked, and take the helmet of salvation and the sword of the Spirit which is the word of God; praying always with all prayer and supplication in the Spirit."

O Lord, strengthen me for the ordeal, give me courage that I do not shrink, and however Thou mayest dispose of me, Thy will be done, for Christ's sake. Amen.

CHAPTER XIX.

IN THE FURNACE.

The day last described was succeeded by a tranquil night. Satan had been once more repulsed and was quieted for a little season. By the grace of God my fears were all removed. I realized now that the Lord was supporting me, and decided that I would approach my dear father as soon as possible. The gracious promises of the divine word seemed to harmonize, concentrate and enter fully into my immediate experience. The Lord fortified my soul for the approaching tornado. Again the next night, there was afforded me another tranquil season of rest. I dreamed of bliss, perfect and permanent. The Lord had given me a victory over Satan, I felt very calm. When I awoke in the morning, it was disappointment that I yet lived. Still my faith in God was steadfast. O, how I loved my blessed Saviour and every one whom He loved.

I am ready now. This very day must settle the question, whether my dear, aged father should know that his son is a Christian: this very day perhaps will seal my earthly fate. I knew no fear now: my pulse beat as easily as my conscience reposed. The unyielding truth of the faithful Saviour prompted me to take my stand on open ground without further delay. "Whosoever shall confess me before men, him will I confess also before my Father which is in Heaven."

The day was Saturday, the Jewish Sabbath. According to law, all business must be suspended. My father's custom, however, was to continue operations all day; but himself and family went to the synagogue. On that morning, father roughly asked me, "Are you going to shule, synagogue, sir?" No sir, I respectfully replied. In answer I received a look of unutterable scorn, which seemed to bespeak the most sovereign contempt. I knew the meaning of it, and rejoiced in the Lord that I deserved it.

Being left to myself, I repaired to the warehouse and waited in intensely painful anxiety for his return: I was impatient to unburden my soul. After a few hours, the entire family arrived. The ladies passed me without remark, and retired to a private show-room. My father was pacing the floor, and the opportunity for me had thus arrived.

"Now is your time," sounded a voice. "Hold, stop, not yet," broke in another. "Embrace the golden moment," trumpeted conscience. "Remember what you will suffer for it," roared the devil. For a minute I was staggered, but the Spirit of God helped me. Faith sheltered my head with her wings. My ever-blessed Jesus, I ruminated; and in a moment I stood firmly and calmly on the floor, facing my dear parent. He scowled at me. Father, ventured I, I have found the Messiah of whom Moses and the prophets wrote. He is Jesus of Nazareth.

O my dear father, I love Him; and you will be lost if you don't love Him too."

It is done. A heavy load broke loose from my heart, and rolled down the hill I had been so very long climbing. There I stood. Now what next? God knows; I cannot divine. For several minutes father stood motionless, gazing on me in speechless surprise. At last he broke the horrible silence by pronouncing a deep-toned curse upon my soul. Being a man of violent temper, he raised his voice to a high pitch.

"Now I know what has been the matter with you for the past nine or ten months"—and raising his voice, he frantically screamed, "You're going to turn Christian, Christian, Christian; you'll go to hell, to hell, to hell." And as he lowered his voice, uttering the same deep curse, he finished by darkening the frown with which he beclouded me in the morning. Rushing past me, up stairs he flew to tell the ladies the astounding news.

True to their prejudice, down they came, screaming like panthers. "May sudden death seize you, you villain," shouted my father. "May you be hanged like the 'crucified one,' and afterward sent to hell," was my step-mother's greeting. "He is drunk," quoth my younger sister; and away she ran and brought a decanter of liquor. Thrusting it in my face, "Here," she continued, "drink more and die."

Just then my brother came in, and if he had had a thousand ears, every tympanum would have rung as they all rushed forward at once to tell him that his brother was a "Meshumut" (turn-coat.) His face turned red, his eyes flashed rage, as he looked at one and then another, to catch the confused narration. Now he is filling up; malice swells to the brim. He darts a look at me, anon at them, burning with indignation. All at once he bursts. Raving and foaming with oaths, he calls upon God to damn my soul. True to his habit of life when choking with rage, he blindly mistakes, damning his own eyes, then his own soul, and only by way of change treating me occasionally to the same brotherly volley. To vary the proceeding, he picked up an old slipper, and throwing it at my head, struck me. "There, take it, you fool, you will need it; it won't be long before you will creep about the street barefoot, begging your bread."

My elder sister, who up to this time had been fastened to the spot, tongue-tied with surprise and anger, at length gave vent to her pent-up passion. With flashing eyes, forgetful that she was a woman, she cursed me with a deep and bitter curse, swearing by a most cruel oath, that "if ever I ate another meal in her presence, she would contrive some way to poison me."

All this time I am standing on the same spot where I first accosted my father. I had no disposition to hide. When, however, one of them gave me a rude push, calling me an automaton, I promptly moved away from them. My dear father retired to the counting-house to confer with his Gentile clerk, who was a wretched infidel. He of course opposed me, and thus added fuel to the fire of my persecution.

"And now, Lord, what wait I for? my hope is in Thee."

It was done: I had openly confessed my Saviour; the spell was broken. Satan frowned, but Jesus smiled. What now could I do but retire to my room, and on my knees give glory to the Lord? Toward evening I went home, and on entering, encountered a scene which will ever be indelibly stamped upon my memory.

My father was sitting on a chair with his head resting upon the table, and audibly sobbing. The family standing around and leaning over, dropped their tears upon him. My heart was stirred. *One kind word from my father then, might have proven fatal to me.*

But it must not be thus. In a moment my step-mother shrieked out, "May God Almighty strike you dead, you villain. Look at the tears you cause your father and us to shed!" My brother was quieted down considerably. With streaming eyes sighed he, "Jonas, I would rather see your corpse at my feet than have you turn Christian." All at once the spirit of the very devil seized him: true, he wept, but for very revenge. "The dread of being hung at the 'Old Bailey,' as a murderer, alone deters me," gnashed he, "from blowing out your brains." In chimed my sisters. "Get out of the room," screamed they; "may your mother's ghost haunt you, and your dead grandmother terrify you in the night." "Send him out of my sight! Shut the door on him!" commanded my father. I understood my *vision* now. I am walking between the fiends unharmed: they cannot hurt me. My bitterest foe is my dear father.

How truthfully has the wise man said, "The heart knoweth its own bitterness, and a stranger doth not intermeddle with its joy." Thus with heart aching exquisitely, and eyes turned to fountains of tears, (and I sought not to restrain these,) for the blindness of my loved ones at home I breathed the prayer, "Father forgive them, for they know not what they do." With this I left the house. I thought that I was now out of that house forever; but no, for my brother came immediately after me, and considerably softened down, suggested that I return to the house and go down into the kitchen with the servants. "Perhaps," reasoned he, "you may change your opinion." So taking from me the keys of the warehouse, he told me to lodge at home, and he would go to the warehouse. I at once acceded. Never since that time have I stepped foot into the room where I obtained for the first pardon for my sins!

That night was a tranquil one for me. I slept securely under the blessing of a clear conscience. The morrow being "Lord's day," I went openly to church, and heard Rev. John Peacock again preach the glorious gospel of Jesus Christ; and never from my birth had I enjoyed such tranquility of mind and serenity of soul.

The discourse was directed to afflicted saints, and gave me great comfort. I left the sacred place with joyful heart, thanking God and taking courage.

Once more on the walk, I realized that I had no

home to go to. Would my father's door be shut against me if I should go there? To decide this question I must put it to test. Entering the house as usual, I was soon made sad by a repetition of the scene of the preceding night. "Where have you been, meshumut (turn-coat)?" To the Christian church, I frankly replied. All eyes were riveted on me. "You," came the chorus, "you and the Christians will all go to hell together." So it went. I ate my dinner at the table in bitterness and silence, hearing all their ribaldry and blasphemy, returning not a single reply.

On the next day I made a visit to Mr. Peacock, and had a most delightful season of religious intercourse with him. Again I wished to be baptized, but was advised to delay in consequence of my delicate situation just then at home. I asked him if it would be my duty voluntarily to leave my father's house? "No," he replied, "for that would be the same as making your own cross, and with your own hands placing it upon your own shoulders." Thus we talked together a long time in smiles and tears. His final counsel was, "Stand still and see the salvation of the Lord." He then offered a special prayer, and as he blessed me, I left his pious house.

This interview inspired me with fresh courage in the cause of Jesus. Every day I grew "in grace and in the knowledge of our Lord and Saviour Jesus Christ." I talked freely to everybody who would hear me, and made the Testament my constant private companion. The family, however, observing that I was growing bold in the expression of my new religion, fanned the persecution against me into increased severity. Yet by grace I was enabled to exercise humility.

Several months previous I had gathered together my wicked books, and as soon as I had found Christ, my precious Saviour, I burned them all. My relations now placed over me a most critical watch. Every movement was remarked upon. They seemed to dread something supernatural. So severe were they, that they filched from me any book they could find. My Testament they could not obtain. They locked up all my clothes, took away my jewelry, and stopped my weekly allowance of money. This looked like the beginning of poverty.

A short time afterward, my dear father made a dispassionate speech to me. "Now, sir, I want you to know that you are a disgrace to my family. You have forsaken your God, to worship a blasphemer and vile robber who was hanged. You call yourself a Christian, consequently you have cut yourself off from your family privileges. Hereafter I forbid you to eat in my presence. Neither shall you sit in the same room with my family. Your place henceforth must be in the cellar-kitchen, *unless you recant.* If you return to your God, and curse this Nazarene, I'll make you rich. In due time you shall have a share in my business, and at my death I'll leave you more than your portion. You have been a good, honest boy all your life, but now you are worse to me than no son at all. Take time to consider my proposition. If you reject my terms, you must expect the worst. Now leave me, and never let me see your face in the parlor again until you recant. Go down stairs and live with the servants!"

During this harangue, several member of the family were present, appearing to enjoy it greatly; and at its conclusion, I was compelled to submit to my lot beneath their jibes and sneers. In a minute I was below in the kitchen with the Gentile servants. A very few words from them assured me of their sympathy. Although they belonged to a class whose lives are always hard-pressed, and who, before these days of reformatory measures for that particular class of women in England, found it difficult to live by honest labor, so as to steer clear of periods of infamy, yet these two women, Mary and Martha, at least were secure through the protection they found in the restraining influence of the Christian religion.

We soon found an opportunity to talk over affairs, when I forthwith produced the stolen Testament, and delivered it over to its rightful owner. The scene that ensued may not even be imagined. Surely I cannot describe the superior brilliancy of that subterranean kitchen, and the holy refinement possessing that low society after I had told my story. Ignorant as they were, they loved the Christian religion, they loved my soul. They now laughed and wept, and sang. Then both put their honest arms around me; enthusiastically they kissed me, and said, "Be of good cheer." Mary told all about her trouble concerning the Testament. Quite superstitious, she thought that "the Devil had fritted it away." "But it's all right now; I've got it back again, and it's converted my young master to Christianity since it's been gone."—Christ was in that kitchen; and the cudgel raised against me, fell harmless upon my head, while every passing moment assisted to bind me closer to the cross.

Thus far I knew nothing about *denominations* of Christians. I wanted congenial society. I loved my Saviour, and desired to be united with His followers. When I went abroad, I was happy in their company; but on every return to my father's kitchen I met trouble. Not a day passed without an effort, made by different Jewish persons, to reclaim me. Threats, bribes and blows were alternately resorted to, but argument never. My brother would reach my heart when at times he threw his arms around my neck, dropped tears on my shoulder, and sobbed out, "*must* we part?" But if I then attempted to say a word to him about Messiah, he grew angry in a moment, rudely saying, "I want none of Him." In another instant he would be just as dead to all sympathy, except that which sensitively contemplated exclusively earthly prospects. From this platform he would deal out his invectives plentifully. ",Fool that you are," judged he, "you are standing in your own light, you are blind to your own interest. Now you may be respected and rich. Father is growing old, he will soon die," (he lived nearly twenty years longer) "and then this property will be yours." Softening down, he would now resort to begging, entreating me to recant, yet intermingling threats. "O do recant! Father has taken an oath" (this he did twenty times every day!) "that if you will not recant, he will disinherit you, kick you out of his house, and shut his doors against you forever. You will then be poor and despised by everybody. and how are you going to live? You are not used to work. You will *starve to death in the 'work-house.'* You will wander up and down the streets bare-foot, and beg your bread from door to door. Then I will spurn you. I'll shun you, and refuse to give you even through Gentile servants, a morsel from my door. The Christians too will hate you, for nobody loves a traitor. Remember your mother who gave you birth; she worshipped our God. Remember your grandmother, who raised you in the same faith. They both died in the Jewish religion, and are now in heaven. If you now become a 'meshumut,' you will be a traitor to them and their God; their ghosts will mock you by day, while you are begging your bread from door to door, and terrify you at night, when you are lying on your pallet of straw. You are breaking your father's heart, and he too will soon die. See my tears! Look to your own interest! Save your property, and live easily." Then he would bend to coaxing, putting his arm around my neck. "O come, my only, dear brother, come back again to our bosoms, and you shall yet be rich."

Here he becomes entirely exhausted. What more should he say? He can offer no other inducement for me to recant. So he would tack about, and work himself mad at the Christians, who were sealing my ruin. Instantly I was deafened by a volley of blasphemies against my blessed Saviour. It was more than I could bear. "Give me argument," protested I. "D— the argument." To all his soft words in my behalf I became invulnerable, the instant one blasphemy was uttered against my glorious Redeemer. Poor fellow! he was zealous for my recantation, but he paid no respect to the most common-place truth, if he could only thereby succeed in striking the smallest spark of hope for my recovery. More than once he told the family that he had well nigh prevailed upon me to recant. Yet when they saw that I was still a Christian, their malice was vented in full measure. In this manner I lingered, chained to a dead body, for several weeks. O how I longed to be unclothed that I might be clothed, effectually clothed with the salvation of Jesus. Thus far nobody had ventured to open the Bible with me. But, to curse Jesus and die, every one seemed ready.

One day my trials were peculiarly severe, on account of the number of persons that constantly assailed me. All their words were alike malicious. A cloud impends; I feel totally discouraged. I do not doubt; but it is growing very dark. Amid my meditation, lo, here comes poor, dear father toward me, for the first time since he banished me from his presence. What does he want? I looked at him sharply, expecting evil from him. But no, I have misjudged; tears are in his aged eyes. He weeps freely. Close to me—I now in his arms—he weeps over me, begging me to recant and return to the God of Abraham. I could not speak. It would have been useless if I had spoken. And, although not stoical, I could not even weep. My father's tears! How *can* I resist these? Ah, now I know how. He pleads with me to curse my blessed Jesus!

But look! see how his tears fall on me. O, my heart, my heart, it swells to bursting. Still I cannot shed a tear. My brain became fevered and my body trembled. Satan flew aloft, and overshadowed me with his black wings. Not a word could I yet speak to my sobbing parent. He spoke kindly to me. Never before did I know how much I loved my dear father. Now he has left me. My brain reels. Retiring to my chamber, the horizon was so cloudy, that I clapped my hand to my forehead, and rashly condemned the whole scene as delusion. Christ, methought, is after all an impostor. Why all this suffering? There is no God, no Devil, no Judgment, no Eternity. Then why this anguish? Death, come to my relief! At the impulse of the moment, I seized a razor, and opened it. Now death, relieve me. Jesus interfered. A death-like, agonizing shudder seized me. I saw death, and was terrified. So great was my alarm, that I dashed the murderous weapon across the room, and looking at the shattered instrument, lying upon the floor, I was forcibly reminded that " no murderer hath eternal life abiding in him."

I was " cast down but not forsaken." This state of mind continued several days; still I had not the most distant idea looking toward recantation. At length, in God's own time, when His gracious purposes were fully matured in me, the clouds began to disperse and gradually unveiled the ethereal blue of the expanse of God's love above my head. While again meditating upon my situation, I seemed to be standing upon the brink of hell, fearlessly sporting with death. At a short distance from me stood my insulted Saviour, holding out touching inducements to draw me from that place and bring me to Him for protection. Thus I am just learning how to make profitable use of His sacred word. "Come unto me, all ye that labor and are heavy laden, and I will give you rest. Take my yoke upon you and learn of me, for I am meek and lowly in heart; and ye shall find rest unto your souls: for my yoke is easy and my burden is light." For a while I remained looking at my position, and thinking about my Saviour's loving words. Brighter with each passing thought my sky became, until I was overcome by the "beauty of the Lord." Then I fled to the Throne of Grace, and poured out contrition as only bitter tears can vent it. Glory to the Lord, the Devil ceased to tempt me. I am learning how to resist him, and he flees from me, leaving me once more firm "in the liberty wherewith Christ hath made *me* free."— Grant, blessed Saviour, that I may never, never again be entangled "in the yoke of bondage."

14

CHAPTER XX.

THE RELEASE.

More than two months have now passed since the events last recorded. Many and furious were the fiery darts of the enemy, but my weapons were indeed powerful, or as a minister of Jesus has expressed it, "The weapons of our warfare are not carnal, but mighty through God to the pulling down of strongholds." I am learning how to wield the sword of the Spirit. I know a little of the unfathomable grace of God which, having sustained me thus far, enables me at this period to reject every bribe for recantation, and to "press toward the mark for the prize of the high calling of God in Christ Jesus."

The month of ——, 1833, had arrived, when God in mercy had determined to "shorten those days" of literal tribulation. It was on a certain Friday that my dear father had been laboring hard with me, vainly endeavoring to provoke me to renounce my Saviour. I need not here repeat much of the conversation, (if it may be so-called,) but the nearest approximation to intelligent reasoning that dear father arrived at, was when he informed me for the first time in my life, (unless he may have blurted it out in some terrible passion) "You have nothing to

do about your sins : *I alone am responsible for you.*"
But father, rejoined I, you forget that I am past
"B'mitzvo." His patience at this was exhausted, so
having given me neither reason nor argument, in the
absence of these he must necessarily foam with madness. "Now, sir," affirmed he, " I'm a-going to put
a stop to so much religion." Supposing that what
he designed to do was yet future, I moved a few
paces away, collectedly to await the result. Nor had
I long to wait. The spirit of persecution, already
present, was only increasing in intensity. My own
dear parent, had he dared, could have equalled either
the ecclesiastic Bonner, or Mary his queen, in severe
and bloody measures. " Come back here, you sir,"
he called to me. I turned to obey, but he was approaching me. He met me half way, but not for
compromise.

Folding his arms, he sneered upon me. " Christian, meshumut, fool, beggar, you might make yourself rich. Stubborn fool that you are, why do you
persist in your present course?" Then he rattled
money in his pocket with one hand, and his watch
seals with the other, taunting me meanwhile for being poor. When satisfied with that part of his pro-
gramme, straightening himself, he raised his voice
to a high pitch. " Hear me, sir, I will give you until *to-morrow night* to make up your mind finally
whether you will recant or not. If you will, I will
be more than a father to you; but if you will not,
I'll turn you out of doors, and cut you off with a
shilling. Then you may go to hell with your
Christians." " So he turned and went away in a

rage." And I "rehearsed it in the ears of the Lord."

The next morning I arose early, and left the house before breakfast, thinking to shun my infuriated father one day, as I supposed that he would go to the synagogue. I did not believe that he would put his threats into execution as soon as he had said. Desiring quietness, I repaired to the warehouse, not expecting to see any of the family until the after-part of the day, and perhaps not at all, that day being Sabbath. I had been there, however, but a few minutes ere my father confronted me. He declared that he was determined to carry out his threats, and that, therefore, I might now look out. Maddened by the thought that he had to come to the warehouse after me, especially on the holy day (?), he commenced swearing awfully at me. That done, what next? "Now, sir," ordered he, "take your place at that corner of the warehouse," pointing to it; "there stay until ten o'clock to-night. Make up your mind by that time what you intend to do." He left me hastily to go, I thought, to the synagogue. I was alone. It was now optional with me either to obey my father or leave the house. I remembered what Mr. Peacock had told me, and resolved accordingly to take my place in the gloomy recess and spend the entire day in prayer and fasting.

My dear brother was really afflicted on my account. He did not go to the synagogue, but in a short time arrived at the warehouse. Hurriedly he advanced toward me, and burying his face in his handkerchief, he wept aloud. I looked on him in

pity and wept too. "Jonas, do recant." How can
I forsake my blessed Saviour? "He is only an impostor," emphasized he. O no, no, I love my very
Redeemer. "'Tis nothing but infatuation," he insisted. No, no, my brother, it is not infatuation.
Jesus is Messiah according to the scriptures, and I
have besides the evidence in my soul. Poor boy, he
was ignorant of both scripture and experimental evidence. What then could he do or say other than
grow angry. Again he portrayed the misery that
would ensue upon my being turned out of doors.
"To-night," urged he, "father will decide your case
against you unless you recant, and you will perish in
the streets. O, how can you be so blind to your
own interest? Do recant! Shall I tell father that
you have recanted? O my *dear* brother, *may* I say
that you have recanted?" He stood over me, seeking to persuade, threatening, entreating, coaxing and
bribing so long (most of the time in tears) that once
I caught myself upon the very verge of yielding to
his brotherly importunities. But, "God is our refuge and strength, a very present help in trouble."
With such a very present help, I was enabled to
plant myself upon the promises of scripture and
stand firm. Failing in his kind effort, he left me,
looking very sad. In a short time he returned with
a message purporting to have come directly from
father. He laid down before me a package of bank-
bills, swearing that if I would recant, this large
amount should be immediately put into my hands.
For a moment I was staggered. I might have played
the hypocrite. My whole "living" was before me

and at my immediate disposal. I might have reached out greedy hands, and have grasped mammon. But here again the Lord spoke. "Lay not up for yourselves treasures on earth." What, must I give up Jesus for so *little?* Go away from me and let me alone, for miserable comforters are ye all. "Fool," thundered he, "let the worst come upon you. Then who will pity you, or care for you? Not I, never."

In an hour or two, my dear father arriving, came and stood within a foot or two of where I was. His countenance changed from contempt to revenge. He looked at me long and steadily. A kind parent, he keenly felt that I was his dependent son. I saw his countenance change to pity. Saying not a word, he turned to leave me; but first fell the blinding tear from his eye. My glance followed him to the counting room. O, why did not he say someting? I had rather felt his wrath, than to have seen that silent tear. I could not bear this; I bowed my head and wept. Here again was Satan's opportunity.

"See what anguish you are causing your dear, kind father, and consider too what anguish he will 'use you in return." This temptation had well h the desired effect. My dear father again in tears for me! What a wretch I am. My soul was cast down; and more than once I actually stepped out of my prison, to sign my recantation and ask my father's forgiveness. Something arrested me. What was it? "He weeps because you will not disown your Saviour, and with himself go to hell. Enter into life halt or maimed, rather than, having two hands or two feet, be cast into everlasting fire."

The thought seemed a present inspiration. It aroused and strengthened me, and blessed be the name of the Lord, I became firmer than ever.

A short time later my step-mother and sisters arrived, dressed in their Sabbath-day gaudy costumes, bedecked with jewelry and feathers, so profuse that it occurred to me at once that they had strained a point for the occasion. I expected to hear from them something not very eloquent. I had heard them "argue" once before. *They* could not move me. They were ignorant and proud. When they persecuted me, the very Devil threw a wet blanket over their womanhood. It was indeed making untoned "trumpets out of flutes, sun-flowers of violets." I pitied them; beyond that I was insensible. Stalking along, they drew up near to where I stood.—Near, I say, for juxtaposition to me in my distress would have been to them as "uncleanness." First they twittered, then sniggered, then grinned; then satirizing, they reached their native element, slang. "Christian," "Christian thief," "fool." "You'll suffer, you rascal;" "you'll repent of all this;" "you'll die in the workhouse and then go to hell." The conclusion was a malediction, unanimously adopted, a "meshonmeshina," sudden death. I was considerably enlightened by their "arguments." They threw light certainly upon Jer. xvii: 9. Their farce ended, exeunt omnes. Disgusted to loathing I turned my back upon them as they were preparing to leave me, and renewed my vow of fidelity to my ever precious Redeemer.

Several times during the day I was sorely tempted

to recant. But after each temptation, I was favored with such clear views of God's eternal, glorious, saving grace, and the word of His truth, that my strength was greatly increased. I was repeatedly constrained to thank God and take courage.

About five o'clock in the evening, the Devil ceased to tempt me. The grace of God proved sufficient. My soul was calm and I glorified my Saviour. New strength given to me, I felt prepared for the final struggle. So established was my determination to suffer for my Lord and Saviour, that I could then have endured (so far as I could judge) the utmost torture of faggot and fire rather than to have flinched from my vow of fidelity to my precious Saviour. Men, women, and demons had left me to my fate. Jesus kept me constant company, blessing me with a serene mind, preparatory to the ordeal that must be passed at ten o'clock that night. I almost prayed for the worst, for I then felt ready to meet it.

It was after nine, when the last of the hands was paid off. The books locked up as usual, the clerk went home, the boy turning off all the gas lights but one solitary burner, turned low. "Now," resumed Satan, "prepare to die." I was already prepared; I expected a death blow, and felt firm as a rock. Let it come, I petitioned, let it come: O God, support me still.

At or about the hour of ten, I was alone with my father, locked up in that warehouse, the key being in his pocket. He took his position at the opposite end of the room, and summoned me to appear before him. In an instant a thought, like an inspiration from the Lord, presented to my mind how my Saviour behaved Himself when He stood before Pilate. I heard a voice say, "Keep your Master, Christ, before you as a pattern." I understood that I must own my Lord, whatever the result. So I obeyed the summons and presented myself before my father. How firm my step! I knew no fear. For a few minutes we simply looked at each other; not a whisper escaped us. Presently he began to mock and deride me. "What do you look like?" But he furnished his own and a most truthful reply—(I felt like smiling.) "You look like what you are, a *Christian*." Then passion flamed up. With loud voice he demanded, "Well, sir, are you willing to part with me?" You, sir, I replied, have ever been to me a good father. You know that I love you. But you know also that for exercising the liberty of choosing my own religion, I don't deserve this persecution. If I am wrong, why don't you sit down with me, and opening our own Bible, show me my error. When thus I am convinced that I am wrong, I'll recant certainly. "You, sir," returned he, "have nothing to do but what I tell you; and I shall be answerable in the day of judgment for you." Oh father, I exclaimed, that may all be rabbi, but it is not Bible. "Tell me, sir," he roared, "would you rather part with me, or with your Christ?" I am ready to make ten thousand sacrifices, even of you, greatly as I love you, and of all that you are worth; but I will never, never part with my Saviour: you can't take from me my Saviour, impossible.

On hearing these words, he cried, he screamed with very madness. He tried to speak, but his passion choked him, and throwing himself across a large mahogany counter, he sobbed like a whipped child. All at once, the furies seizing him, he jumped up, cursing and running toward me with uplifted umbrella—the only thing at hand. "Tell me once for all," he thundered, "are you a Christian?" I am, leaped from my mouth. At this he cursed my soul repeatedly. "Now go to the Christians, and see if they will give you one meal's victuals." He then seized the collar of my coat, and kicked me all the way out of the house. Locking the door and coming up to me, he thrust his clenched fist close to my face, and again cursed my soul with most horrid cursings. He wished me in the burning flames of hell, crying at the same time, "—— your soul; you'll repent this."

"The Lord knoweth the way of the righteous." Jesus saw me. I heard angels sing with voices full of heavenly melody, "when my father and my mother forsake me, then the Lord will take me up." I was emboldened. I felt courageous. In a loud voice, I said, Father, I shall never, never repent this step; but you will.

CHAPTER XXI.

GOD WILL PROVIDE.

The Rubicon passed, leaves my life still my own. True, I am hurled down from affluence to poverty; but the mystery that I still live, for a short time at least absorbs every other thought. When one thus hangs upon moments of time, hovering between life and death, thoughts travel with wonderful velocity. In rapid succession events in retrospect passed before me. There come to my mind many truths, both elevating and mysterious. But here, right before my eyes, stands with living evidence the greatest mystery that I had yet encountered. My father has deserted me! With scowl and curse he turned upon his heels, leaving me standing on the street after night, spell-bound to the same spot for several minutes, wondering at the wickedness of that religion which could so harden my dear father's heart as to drive him from his *vow to my dead mother*, and from all sense of natural obligation to his son, because that son loved liberty of conscience and could not suffer himself any longer to be chained down by bigotry, prejudice, and a worn-out religion. But thus it was.

For the first time in my life, I am without a bed to lie upon. My clothes are shabby, the pockets nearly empty. My next meal was as far off as my bed. Nor was there a living being on earth that I knew of, to whom I could confide *all* my situation, except the poor boy Thomas; but he was fully sixty miles distant. Besides, he had once said that he could not help me when my distress came. Neither could I, even under the present circumstances, consent to beg my bread of him or any other living being. No, Jesus has said, every one that hath forsaken houses, or brethren, or sisters, or father, or mother, or wife, or children, or lands, for my name's sake, shall receive a hundred fold, and shall inherit everlasting life. Here, then, I claim a positive, a specific promise. I may weep a little in my loneliness, nay, if it be God's will that I starve, so be it. But, " *beg my bread from door to door*," I never will. True, just at this stage, an inquisitive tear ventured to peep out of its hiding place, just to inquire, " what's the matter?" but the wet little busy-body was quickly dried off and thrust aside. No, God my friend; I *will* NOT beg!

Did I yearn after the flesh pots? I would not exchange conditions with my brother or father. Still mechanically I turned my face toward my former home, and musingly walked until I stood opposite the well-known, elegant dwelling. I looked in at a window where I could see company in full dress at the card tables. All was merriment. One heart was without, cast down but not forsaken. I could easily have entered; the two servants would have assisted me. What, beg my bread at my father's door? Never! Then there is no admittance for me. I can bear to be thrown on faith, with a heavy heart too. Was my faith weak? I turned away and resolved to seek admittance into the warehouse. A solitary walk of two long miles, and I halted. The dreary place was locked up and dark. Who sleeps there? My brother? I'll arouse him up and beg for admission. O God, my brother's prophesy, shall it ever come true? God, my helper, *never*. There remained for me but one alternative, to lie down upon a door-step, thus running the risk of being locked up by the police. I reasoned, that should this take place, all the facts would soon be made public, and perhaps this, therefore, is the way the Lord intends to make provision for me. But, as the heaven is high above the earth, so great is His mercy toward them that fear Him; as far as the East is from the West, so far He hath removed our transgressions from us. Like as a father pitieth his children, so the Lord pitieth them that fear Him : for He knoweth our frame; He remembereth that we are dust. Thus it will be seen directly, that my gracious Saviour had already made provision for me, but I did not know it. He had also opened a way for publicity to be given, not only less mortifying to my weak nature, but more honorable to His own glorious cause. Man's extremity is indeed God's opportunity, as was fully verified in my case.

A feeling of resignation seemed to pervade my soul. I was ready to submit to any result of the Lord's arranging. So astonishingly contented did I feel, that I remember lightly soliloquizing as I surveyed my proposed stony bed preparatory to lying down for the night. I don't know which is the soft side of this bed, but my Master had it just as hard, so here goes. I start to lie down, when a hand is laid upon my shoulder. The police? Any way will do. Recovering from the momentary shock, my surprise was increased by the appearance of a young man at my side, apparently about my own size and age, looking at me with a very anxious expression. "Are you in trouble, sir?" he asked. I am. "Is your trouble for Christ's sake?" It is. "What is the nature of your trouble?" he continued. This night I have left all to follow Christ, my Saviour. "Well, well," chimed in he, "my mother has been in trouble about something ever since four o'clock this afternoon. She has had an impression on her mind that she must relieve some child of God. And now, if you are in want of a home to-night, come with me. I have a bed to lie on, and you shall share it with me."

I could not reply; my heart rose to my throat. Struck dumb with wonder and amazement at the extraordinary way of the Lord, gratitude riveted a mind admiring the goodness of my blessed Saviour who had saved me from the horrid mortification of begging my bread from door to door. Locking arms with me at once, "Come," confided he, "let us go home." In meekness and silence, I suffered him to lead me. We soon arrived at the house, when he introduced me to his mother. "Here he is, mother, the Lord has sent him." The widow was sitting before the fire, and her large Bible lay open on her knees. She looked at me through her spectacles,

and inquired, " Are you a Christian, young man?"
I am. "Are you in need of a home?" I am.
" Come," and she drew me to her, " sit down and
tell me your story." It was done as she requested.
I was not surprised to see tears in the eyes of this
pious woman, but venturing to look about me upon
the strangers, I did wonder when I saw every one of
them weeping. " Well, well," explained she, push-
ing her spectacles to the top of her head, " about four
o'clock this afternoon I opened my Testament, and
the very first passage that my eye fell upon was He-
brews xiii: 2." Pulling down her " specs," she
pointed with her finger and read " Be not forgetful
to entertain strangers, for thereby some have entertained angels unawares." " I have," she added,
" been strongly exercised in mind from that hour
until now. I could not go to bed, my desire for
sleep all left me; and not one of the family would
go, until I felt satisfied what was the ' will of the
Lord.' George, my son, suggested I, walk out
awhile, and it may be the Lord will direct you to
some worthy stranger. I did not dream that ' an
angel' would come into my house, but I did expect
a human being; and now the Lord has sent you to
me for protection, and He has told me to provide a
home for you. Now put your trust in Jesus: the
Lord has taken you up, and I will be to you as a
mother." Hitherto my heart beat, but my eyes were
amazingly dry until this last word, mother. In a
moment, I broke down, only gasping, O God of the
widow.

It was midnight. No noon-day sun shone with

more glorious brightness than my heart emitted within me at that hour. "Come," said George, taking my hand, "let us go to bed." We bowed down upon our knees and talked with God. On arising, George again took my hand, and looking me directly in the eye, "Remember," repeated he, "'the foxes have holes, and the birds of the air have nests, but the Son of Man hath not where to lay His head.'" Then pausing for a moment, he supplemented with emphasis, "but we have." I turned into bed with overflowing heart. My pillow felt downy. Sleep I could not, but I could anticipate the coming morning with tears of gratitude and words of joy.

Nearly three weeks of uninterrupted tranquility did I enjoy under this benevolent, Godly roof. Every hour I grew stronger in the grace of God. It was deemed advisable that I should remain secluded for a while, so my relations did not know my whereabouts. Meanwhile their movements were closely watched, as they were prowling about and inquiring for me in every direction, as though they were in quest of prey. Some time afterward, I was told that my father had expended considerable money for the purpose of kidnapping me, to lodge me in a private mad-house. But the Lord was my protector, and he failed.

Soon as it was known to my father that I was cared for by the Christians, he sent me daily bribes, urging me to recant. Failing, he resorted to harsh measures, and threatened to prosecute the widow for harboring me, pleading that I was a minor. This raised up very many friends for the widow and in my behalf, who, as an offset, threatened my father with suit for my support, upon the ground that he had thrown me out of a home and refused to give me shelter under his roof, while I was a minor.

This condition of things grieved me very sorely. I could not bear the prospect of bringing into serious collision my Christian friends and Jewish foes. I could do naught other than I had done, but I never calculated upon drawing others into trouble on my account. And now that it actually came, it was more than I could bear. I fell into a desponding state of mind, of which the Devil took the greatest advantage; such indeed that well nigh I lost sight of the mercies of God and rushed heedless of results into eternity. For I was on the eve of attempting suicide a second time! "Hang yourself," darted Satan, "and have done with this trouble. Go on; you are a Jew still, and, therefore, you are perfectly secure. Or if you are a Christian, you must in any event be damned, unless you are of the 'predestinated' few. Hang yourself, and so end your trouble."

The terrible arrangements were made and only awaited the final, fatal leap in the dark, when I was interrupted by the hurried approach of the oldest son of the widow, who began at once to talk about my father. There had been an interview with him, held by my friends. Both parties agreed to withdraw their suits, as my father had said that he should give himself no more concern or uneasiness about me, did not care what became of me, that I should never enter into his house again, and that on no account would he pay a single shilling for me. My

15

friends responded that there were Christians enough who would assist me, and so the matter ended. "Now," insisted the young man, "you must be at rest, the difficulty is all settled and we will assist you, so that you will be able to support yourself independently."

I received this as a sovereign balm to my troubled mind, and gradually became tranquil. When I clearly saw how wonderfully the Lord had delivered my soul from death, I blessed His holy name who had frustrated my wicked purpose, and prayed that the name of Jesus Christ might be glorified in all my future life.

CHAPTER XXII.

MESSIAH SYMBOLICALLY WEDDED.

After the events of the last chapter, I found myself in new circumstances and foreign surroundings. For several days I had nothing to do but to think, and I assure you, my reader, that the time was thus improved most industriously. I went over all the ground again, mapped accurately the lay of the land, tested its qualities with the more perfect helps at hand, explored a number of Christian books, tried arguments for and against, and thus arrived at the point of departure, where Jesus unites the East and West, Jew and uncircumcised. I felt satisfied with every step I had taken for my adorable Saviour. But here I am, dwelling under this Christian roof, receiving Christian instruction and breathing a Christian atmosphere. Christians had given me a bed: Christians were feeding me: Christians were encouraging me to persevere. Could my dear father but know how unspeakably serene my mind is, would he say ever again, "You and the Christians will all go to hell together?" Yes, he would. He could not say aught else, as a Jew! Now I see what all my visions meant. I have passed through the ranks of my enemies unscathed. Even my angry father

227

could do no more than impoverish me. I am "light out of darkness," and if God help me, I will "walk in the light." I joyously feel that now I am quite ready to be baptized. I experienced such a sense of freedom in the matter, that smiling I said, "I'm '*B'mitzvo*' now, of a truth."

A day or two later, I visited Mr. Peacock again, and renewed my request for baptism. I was cordially received by the whole family, to whom I confided the history of my situation. Everything that I related, easily understood, was readily received. Many were the kind words that saluted me, and full and valuable the instruction. But after remaining in the house more than an hour, hearing nothing about the baptism I wished, I began to grow restless, fearing that I had made mistake in some way. It must be borne in mind that I had never seen a baptism, and did not know exactly how it was accomplished; only impressed that the person must be "buried" in water, for what length of time I was of course ignorant. At length I ventured to ask again for baptism. The good man expressed his willingness to accommodate me. Addressing his wife, "Jane," quoth he, "bring me a bowl of water, and I'll give Mr. Davis a private baptism." On hearing these words, I pushed back my chair with force against the wall. I must have turned pale, for I felt alarmed at the strange proceedings. "What's the matter, sir?" exclaimed Mr. Peacock. Only I don't understand what you are doing. "I am going to baptize you." What, in a bowl of water? "Yes, why not?" Here I became embarrassed and simply replied, "I must go 'down into' the water, and be 'buried with Christ by baptism.'" "But," interposed he, "you must know that baptism has come in the room of circumcision, and is, therefore, a substitute for that rite; for that reason infants are baptized (which is sometimes called christening,) and this is done, therefore, by sprinkling them. Now, as you have not been christened in infancy, why not be so now?" Unprepared for all this, I felt confused. The minister appeared pleased. Presently, however, an idea inspired me. Mr. Peacock, said I timidly, did you say that baptism was a *substitute* for circumcision? "So it is taught,"said he. Then, I modestly replied, am not I *exempt* from the rite of baptism as a *substitute*, from the fact that I have been *circumcised*, and you can't *uncircumcise* me? Must *I* then have both primitive rite and its mere substitute?

A mischievous smile played at the corner of his mouth, and his wife honestly laughed outright. By this time, I was feeling quite "green." Placing his chair near me, "My young friend," he resumed, "I want to relieve your embarrassment." Here he entertained me for a long time with the history of the Christian church, its denominations, different opinions, etc., assuring me that all Christians, of every human name, were one in heart and equally accepted by the Father through Jesus the Saviour. "I have put you to this test, in order to find out how you, in your unbiased and secluded study of the scriptures, understand the New Testament. I am quite satisfied with you, and will propose you to the church as a candidate for baptism." May I inquire, I asked eagerly, what your church is called? To which he answered, "I am a Baptist, understanding the New Testament as you do, and admitting nothing else. I asked no further questions. I was uneasy to know how baptism was done: but be patient, restless heart.

Shortly after this interview, I was waited upon by a committee from the church, whose business it was to hear me, ask questions relative to my conversion, and then report to the church. Being favorable to my reception as a member, they at once named the time for my appearance before that body. At the time mentioned, I was present, and upon the favorable report, I was voted in as a member, after I should be baptized.

The circumstance of a Jew about to be baptized had a tendency to gather a very large crowd of people on the evening of the ceremony. It must be understood that all the Baptist churches in London have each its own baptistery, well supplied with water. An appropriate discourse was delivered, after which the candidates were invited into the vestry rooms to prepare for the ordinance. O, how exceedingly strange all this appeared to me, but when we returned to the chapel and were marshalled in front of the water, my astonishment knew no bounds. I felt desperately impatient to go into the water, so much so that when the clergyman took the hand of the first convert to be immersed and walked into the water, in my ignorance of proceedings, I followed close behind him. In a minute he saw me. "Stop, stop, a moment," said he, and handed me back again to bide my time. What was the matter with me? the moment I saw the candidate baptized in the name of the sacred Trinity, tears would come. So I "went down into" the consecrated waters which washed away those kindred tears to emerge from my liquid grave as "light out of darkness;" for I left the waters smiling. Now am I a member of Christ's church.

I must here relate some incidents that transpired on the occasion. As I was being led into the water, a voice from the gallery shrieked out, "My brother!" At the same instant a young man, just in the act of throwing himself down upon the crowd beneath, was restrained by those around him, who seizing hold of him as half his body hung over, pulled him back in the greatest possible excitement. I rely upon the story as it was told to me, everybody arriving at the same conclusion, that the young man was my own, my only, dear brother. Appeals, made to me for a solution, I could only answer by presuming that it was my brother. Everybody was the more convinced of that fact by his conduct. He tore himself from the grasp of his many saviors, pushed his way rudely through the crowd, muttering as he moved, "He's gone, he's gone." So he "went away in a rage." The only explanation I could imagine as accounting for that extraordinary circumstance was that the fact of my intended baptism had reached my brother's ears. He still hoping against hope for my recantation, looked upon my present movement as something decisive. He had not believed that I would take the final step and *join* the Christian church. But when he saw me going into the water, he was goaded on to frensy by an evil spirit, and thus in madness he would have become a murderer and suicide, if Christian hands had not saved him. Then, when he saw me immersed in water, in the name of the Father and of the Son and of the Holy Ghost, his last hope blasted, despair seized him, the evidence of this being expressed in his words of anguish, " He's gone! he's gone!"

Fortunately I was insensible to the affair at the time. Nothing, therefore, marred my delight, but a cherished circumstance enhanced it. The moment I " came up out of the water," I was caught in the arms of as handsome a young man as I have since seen. In a loud voice he said, " Brother, in the name of the Lord Jesus Christ, I greet you with a ' holy kiss.'" He then kissed my forehead. That kiss sunk down deep, very deep into my heart; I have never for a moment lost its effect. The young man was a Polish Jew, who had embraced Christianity some time previous. I felt encouraged and strengthened. Making from time to time acquisitions to that strength, during a period of thirty-four years, dating from that sacred night, January 7th, 1834. I continue until this day, by the grace of God, steadfast and faithful to my baptismal vow. " Now also, when I am old and gray-headed, O God, forsake me not; until I have showed Thy strength unto this generation, and Thy power to every one that is to come."

CHAPTER XXIII.

SET ADRIFT.

Go back in mind, dear reader, and recall all that you have read of this narrative, that you may see clearly my present attitude. I have been leading you along the meandering stream of my Christian experience, until at length you behold me enjoying the privilege of membership with the people of God in His militant church. By my Jewish relations, this last step was construed as the death-blow of hope for my recantation. They regarded me now, so far as my membership in the family held out, as *dead*. They buried me in effigy, and went through mimic or real (I know not which) funeral obsequies. I never learned whether they said "Kadesh" for my soul after death, but know that according to the custom of mourning for the dead, they imposed on themselves a seven days' ordeal, sitting upon stools and refusing to be comforted. The men neglected their beards a month, had on shabby clothes, the coat having a rent made in it, and—but why repeat?

There were some attendant circumstances well calculated to upset the entire pantomime. The description of one only must here suffice. My loved ones at home were cursing me with every breath, and affectionately wishing me a " Meshunmeshina," sudden death.   Now, I think that they ought to have received *that* fact as evidence that I was not dead at all.   They pretended to mourn, but in vain.   My father, however, did a very sensible thing.   Soon as he could spare time from cursing my soul, he altered his will so as entirely to disinherit the apostate, and the more effectually to rob me of any lingering hope to repossess myself of a small portion of my rightful share, he at once received my brother into partnership with him in his business.   Thus I was wholly cut off from ever associating with any one member of the family.

In a temporal point of view, I am now poor and dependent.   I have lost all my earthly possessions and friends.   But I "have not yet resisted unto blood," and *have* found the Pearl of great price, my heavenly Treasure, my blessed Saviour, my Friend that sticketh closer than a brother.   A voice whispers, "Fear not; it is I:" and shall I repine for what I have lost?   No, "what things were gain to me, those I counted loss for Christ; yea doubtless, and I count all things but loss for the excellency of the knowledge of Christ Jesus my Lord, for whom I have suffered the loss of all things, and do count them but dung, that I may win Christ."

Notwithstanding my Christian surroundings and entire alienation from my relations, no human arm could have been potent enough to protect a solitary boy from the malice of an infuriated company of bigoted Jews, many of whom knew me and were a source of daily annoyance and petty persecution.   Hence I found it to be necessary that I seclude myself as much as possible. But business on however limited a scale demanded more publicity than I dare venture into. My difficulty in this respect continued to increase to such an extent that *I resolved to quit my native land and seek a home on American soil.*

All my movements must now be directed toward carrying out my plans. Is it weakness for me to confess that I did wish to see my relations before leaving England—perhaps forever? I had been away from home about six months, when one day I met my father on the street, and mechanically grasped his hand. Mistaking me for an associate or fellow tradesman (!) he looked pleased for a moment; but the instant he recognized me, his countenance grew dark, he cursed me as a "meshumut," broke loose from my hold and so passed on. With anguished heart, I gazed after him, sighing the jeremiad, "O that my head were waters and mine eyes a fountain of tears, that I might weep day and night. for the slain of the daughter of my people. O that I had in the wilderness a lodging place of wayfaring men, that I might leave my people and go from them, for they be all adulterers, an assembly of treacherous men."

Time grew. Nine or ten months passed and I had not moved my foot across the threshold of my dear father's house. The thought of leaving the country without once more seeing my relations, continued exceedingly painful. I even dared to dream of a good-bye kiss. I now resolved to break through all restraint, and abruptly enter that place which was once my home. There, yet lived those whom I still loved; and my heart did give out a thrill at the thought of talking, and perhaps weeping with them once more. But my beau ideal dreams of such exquisitely woven silken cords of fraternal affection were never to be realized.

All arrangements for my voyage to New York were completed. I *must* talk to my father once more, face to face. I watched for a good opportunity on a Saturday, when I knew that the entire family would most likely be together at the warehouse, on their return from the synagogue. Such an opportunity soon arrived. On the next Saturday you might have seen your humble servant on the street, walking in the rear of a flashily-dressed group consisting of my father and step-mother in front, two sisters and brother, with their companions, following after, and your aforesaid humble, then very humble servant, volunteer rear-guard. The strangers dropped off to go to their homes, and " our folks " entered the warehouse, I following at their heels, determined to brave it through this time, well knowing that they could do me no more harm. In a moment my sisters and step-mother saw me. A look, a start, a squeal, as if they saw a mouse; an appropriate expression of surprise, that sounds in your ear like " Sh'mong B'nai," (hear, my son!) and then, as if the hogs of Gadara, or their motive power, or both, or the whole kith and kin were after them, up the stairs they scud, looking over their shoulder every leap or two, at me, the adjudged demoniac, until the charming view dissolved, for exeunt omnes. I have no doubt that as soon as they touched bottom, they indulged another appropriate word of surprise, which sounded to the ear uninitiated like "Sh'mong Yesroile," (hear, O Israel!) and then doubtless blessed me with a bitter "Meshunmeshina." I leave them as frightened as though they had seen the ghost of him whom they had pantomimically buried a few weeks previously. Turning around, boldly I followed my father into the counting-house, where I met with a reception commensurate with my former treatment.

The instant he saw me, his brows contracted. "What do you want here?" he demanded. I want, explained I, to take my leave of you, and before I go, see if you still have a father's heart. "You're not my son," he broke forth, and very coarsely asked, "Where are you going?" I am preparing to embark for America, and do not expect to see you ever again, until I meet you at the bar of God. "Are you still a Christian?" he cried. I am. "Go then to America," he rejoined, "and mind, sir, what I now say to you. If you arrive safely in America, and there recant, send me word, and I will provide you with ample means to return home; but if you won't recant, then, whether you are hanged, murdered, drowned, or poisoned, it will not move me, for I don't care what becomes of you; and then, if you ever send me a letter, I will neither read it, nor answer it." May I go up stairs and see the family? I asked. "No," said he, "they don't want to see you ever again." This treatment cut me to the heart, and in spite of my strongest exertions to repress it, a tear would stray forth. However, I had not entered there to weep, but to show courage for Christ's sake. I stretched out my hand toward my father, and my voice raised, with an effort, breathed, "Father, farewell," my right hand still extended. Tardily, begrudgingly his hand moved toward me. With a firm grasp I seized it, holding it with both my hands; then looking him full in the face, *Father*, said I, *farewell forever!* This touched him. In spite of his pride, his eyes filled quite full, and as he gently drew away his hand from me, he muttered, "*Go, and I wish you well.*" As I caught these words my heart almost burst. I turned away from him. Never have I seen him since.

During this scene, my brother, who had evidently seen me at the first, had remained out of sight, but within hearing. But now that I have turned to leave the place forever, I am confronted by my brother, who was standing in the middle of the floor waiting for me. I saw him, and expected another blast. For some time (as it seemed) we stood looking at each other, and almost ere we were either of us aware, without a single word being spoken, we were in another moment locked in each other's arms sobbing aloud.

My time was short. Breaking loose from his hold, I took his hand in mine. "Farewell, dear brother," said I, "farewell—perhaps forever!" He turned from me weeping; and I left the inhospitable place, never to enter it again. I had bid adieu to both father and brother. I had seen their tears, and honored their manhood. My religion taught me to have pity upon them because of their darkening igno-

rance. If I could account the same for the course of
the female part of the family, I should cherish the
more comfortably their memories. Alas, they were
too much hardened to sympathize in the least with
me. Let blushing bury its face, as I rehearse the
astounding fact, that all through this tragedy the
women of my own family were so lost to every tender sentiment, as to treat the whole event with spite-
ful lightness. They did not manifest the least anxiety even for my recovery; but seemingly lost to fem-
inine sensibility, their invectives were harsher, and
their general conduct more cruel toward me than
the men ever dreamed of. Father, forgive them, for
they know not what they do.

The balance of my time must be occupied in giving and taking adieus. Many a Christian prophesied
that one day I should be a minister of Jesus. And
my good old pastor cautioned, "If ever you preach
the gospel, every time you have finished a sermon—
leave off!" The whole church prayed for me, and I
felt blest. I took my leave of M. and her mother.
I might have had company to America, but the Lord
ordered otherwise; and time has proved all the
Lord's arrangements for me to have been well ordered.

CHAPTER XXIV.

ENGLAND, FAREWELL.

I love thee well,
England, my native land;
Thy scenes on every hand
Prized history tell.

Through tunnels dark,
Through forests dense and damp
Has been my weary tramp?
Quenching hope's spark.

So let it be.
Where should the Christ be found,
Where His rich grace abound?—
On Calvary.

My Calvary!
Thou altar mount now green
Whose dew hath been
The sweat of agony.

Yet, Zion blest
Doth neighbor closely by:
Song tunes my every sigh;
Care sinks to rest.

A father dear?
Ah such an one, in heaven!—
And kindred near?
In Christ all these are given.

Still steals the sigh:
Home, where is now my home?
Only in memory—
Rather, in joys to come!

England, farewell;
From thee my fatherland
I've caught, e'en on thy strand,
  A seer's spell.

This effusion of my soul as it poured itself forth at the present juncture, was faithfully expressed and sympathetically worded by another on learning my relish for a morsel of verse, my desire in particular to have thus set forth the tender experiences of this affecting epoch. The approaching change was great. Thirty-four years ago, when I was in my native city, London, it seemed a very long voyage to America, and like reaching earth's jumping-off place to have arrived at New York. But I have since passed through most of the re-united states, while these have multiplied, and are outstripped by steam communication. So now my youthful alarm seems an excellent joke.

But these three decades must be retraced. In a few days I was actually on board of the old whaler, Calista, which was to bear me over the deep to a land of strangers. And here must be my prison, in company with some two hundred others, until it shall please the God of the ocean to dispose of me further.

The reader has doubtless at some time been thrown into society so abhorrent to him that he would instinctively shy off to one side and " meditate." Such is the repugnant company at a country tavern to the refined traveler, who nevertheless cannot better his condition. Worse even as you may imagine it, is the mental tribulation of an innocent man, who wrongfully suspected and consequently arrested, is,

16

of course, thrown into the prison-yard in company
with the lowest felon. How naturally he shrinks to
a secluded corner, there to think—about what?
Aye, "that's the question."

It is well understood that now I am not rich, sufficiently poor indeed to prompt me to take my place
among the poorest emigrants. Still, I felt very happy with Christ in my heart, a true disciple of my
own good old Moses. "When he was come to years
he refused to be called the son of Pharoah's daughter, choosing rather to suffer affliction with the people of God, than to enjoy the pleasures of sin for a
season, esteeming the reproach of Christ greater
riches than the treasures in Egypt; for he had respect
unto the recompense of the reward." Thus my mind
ran on, as thoughtfully (and gloomily) I called up
before my mind's eye all the characters that had
played any part in my drama. The first evening on
board of the ship was my initiatory to a world—mul-
tum in parvo, much in a small space. All were entire strangers to me, and their company was so very
unpleasant, so strikingly contrasted with what I had
been used to, that it required several days' experience
in that ship's hold before I could understand practi-
cally the precept, "Love thy neighbor." You,
therefore, know why I walk the steerage alone.

Every event of the past, present, and probable future rose up before me. I seemed to live several
months over again. Now, I am visiting M.; I see
her before me; she is telling me about " His blood:"
I feel content to listen, since things have turned out
as they have. Now, I reflect on the hard-heartedness

of my female relations, then the obduracy of my
father. Again, I think of the sorrow of my poor
brother, and then of his prophesy about "begging."
Here the question pops up, what shall I do when I
arrive at New York? True, I have a letter from my
church, directed *to any other church of the same faith
and order;* but I may lose that, and I have not a line
to any individual who might be my friend. I feel
gloomy. Perhaps I *may* be a beggar after all.
"The Lord knoweth the way of the righteous."
But here I am, *alone* in the world. Have not I seen
my dear brother for the last time? He at least shall
never see me in this company, or know of my penury
in America. In turn, I grow impatient to be on my
voyage. Any condition is preferable to suspense.
Seated on my trunk, with eyes closed and face buried
in my hands, I do not weep, but simply breathe a
prayer to God, and wait!

Somebody has laid a hand lightly on my shoulder.
There was language in that magnetic touch. I did
not start; I felt no fear of anybody. The hand lingered. I felt it tremble on my shoulder. Raising
my head, I ventured to look at the owner of that
hand. It was my brother! He had come to make
one more effort for my recovery. Neither of us
could speak a word. He appeared stupefied, and
looked confused, and I am confident that he would
have sunk, if he had not laid his head on my shoulder, to weep; and only when he was sufficiently recovered to speak, could he inaudibly sob out, "my
brother! my brother!" His broken sentences for
several minutes I did not understand. I stretched

my arm around him, but I could neither speak nor weep. It was several minutes before he was sufficiently composed to speak. He then made me some valuable proposals to return home, but the proviso to all was that I must recant. He came so sure of success, that he had brought with him a porter to carry back my trunks. But "the love of Christ constrained me." I could not recant: he could not move me. He remained with me until dark, then left, greatly disappointed by his failure.

Next morning, the ship was towed to a watering place about five miles distant. Many of the passengers remained on shore all night. I tarried in the ship, thinking of everything, suppressing an occasional stray tear, but regretting nothing. Arousing to the consciousness that this is all for Christ's sake, I bowed my head in submission to the Lord's arrangements, drew the strap of my armor a little tighter, and felt the power of actual faith.

Day and night are the same to the sailor. Give him light enough and he will work on. All night long there was the confusion of such business as is peculiar to the mariner. Arrangements for a speedy departure were nearly completed by the morning. Passengers and freight were hurrying and being hurried on board. Personally, I was anxious to be gone. I did not want to recognize again forever any one of my relations. Yet I loved them; I did more than that for my brother, I loved and pitied him.

I had now given up my dear, "Old England" and all familiar faces forevermore. I was watching the men with considerable emotion, as their shore labors neared completion, when lo, if the ghost of my dead great-grandfather had been on the rigging of that old whaler, I should not have been more surprised than I was to see standing before me once more my inevitable brother! Moments were flying fast. He talked nervously, and sobbed freely. He did not appear to have brought any special message this time, but he could not control his emotions. "Must you go? Will you leave us? You'll starve in America; nobody will care for you. Your father is almost broken-hearted. He says if you will *only say* yes, *only say*, that you recant, and will come home, that he will be more than a father to you." Then he offered me, as heretofore, bribes of money to elicit my recantation. "I might only say, 'I recant.'" Thus he continued to labor as only a faithful brother knows how to do until the hour had arrived for leaving. The captain's well-known, "Loose her," was responded to by the mate's, "Aye, aye, sir; loose her." Still my brother, agitated in every nerve, clung to me, concernedly looking toward the shore. "O," wailed he, "must I part with my brother? I never knew that I loved you until now. You have got my heart; take it with you, farewell." I drew him close to me and kissed him. Our tears mingled. Brother, I assured him, farewell, farewell. I have "a Friend that sticketh closer than a brother." He will cross the ocean with me, and take care of me in America. "Company off," and one general rush from ship to shore, and the gallant old whaler was before the breeze. Now for the first time I looked at faces on shore. There stood my brother, weeping. My heart bled for him. Here I recognized, as arriving just too late, M. and her mother, with several members of the church. I saw the waving of handkerchiefs. I did not return the salute, for my mind was absorbed by that one handkerchief which shrouded the eyes of my dear, dear brother. Long and lovingly I looked towards the receding shore. Did I look as Lot's wife looked? The Lord my witness, no! "Truly if they had been mindful of that country from whence they came out, they might have had opportunity to have returned. But now they desire a better country, that is a heavenly; wherefore God is not ashamed to be called their God, for He hath prepared for them a city." The figures on shore fade away. Distance dropped the curtain between us, as the last of the summer of 1834 was blessing "Merrie Old England."

> "The path of sorrow, and that path alone,
> Leads to the land where sorrow is unknown:
> No trav'ler ever reach'd that blest abode,
> Who found not thorns and briers on the road."
>
> —COWPER.

CHAPTER XXV.

ON THE OCEAN.

The waters saw Thee, O God, the waters saw Thee; they were afraid,
the depths also were troubled. Thy way is in the sea, and Thy
path is in the great waters. O Lord, how manifold are Thy works!
In wisdom hast Thou made them all: the earth is full of Thy riches. So is this great and wide sea, wherein are things creeping
innumerable, both small and great beasts. . . . They that go
down to the sea in ships, that do business in great waters, these
see the works of the Lord and His wonders in the deep.

Land out of sight, we are now fairly on the ocean!
"Don't you dread going to America?" I don't
know! "Ar'n't you afraid of beggary?" Let me
alone! "Don't you want to go home?" Go away.
I don't feel well. "Now just think——." I can't
think; I'm sick. Let me alone! What's got over
me? I feel, I feel, like; like every one else on board.
That is to say we are all sea-sick. Now, some
"land lubber," who has never smelt salt water, may
read this and wonder what this sea-sickness resem-
bles. It has been often described, yet I have always
thought a person quite gifted who could give an ac-
curate idea of the condition of things in an orchestra
of one hundred and fifty performers giving forth at
the same time, and each one acting his part independently. Imagine yourself as feeling very bilious,
when an invisible hand lays you on the broad of
your back upon the ground. Now you are being

lifted by your feet. Up you go till your head drops down. High in air you are swung swiftly around. Now you are let down gently, and replaced upon your feet, to stand, yes, all alone. Pray, how did you come so? might be asked. In the South, you may remember having seen a flock of ugly turkey-buzzards, ranged along the fence during a very rainy day. Do you remember how miserable they appeared with head, wings, feathers, and *rain* all drooping together? Well, these *creatures* present a *little* picture of distress when compared with one hundred "furriners," all busy together over the ship's sides. This is sea-sickness; and my good feeling for my uninitiated reader is evidenced by the sincere wish that he may purchase all his knowledge in the premises from observation, and not from practice.

Thus it will be readily understood why it was that I was in no danger of being bothered by thoughts of any kind and about anything. With every pulsation most giddily interested in *passing* events, the sufferer only thinks of one event more; and that is, of lying at the bottom of the sea in preference to living (?) on the top of it. Many a time since then, I have dwelt with rapturous contemplation upon the idea given to us through John, in Rev. xxi. 1: "There was no more sea!" As that will be so, I want to live in that beautiful country. Why not? Here we have sea, and if you will read the hundred and seventh psalm, you will find that you cannot "see the works of the Lord, and His wonders in the deep," unless you submit to "stagger like a drunken man." But

yonder there will be "no more sea." Consequently
no such sickness will mar the travel of eternal life.
no geographical boundaries bar social interchange,
no obstruction exist to the family intercourse of all
God's dear children; again, by consequence no sects
will be found, and nothing to disunite men's praises
forever. There the native air will depend upon the
breath of the Lord for its vitality, and not upon the
phenomena of ocean: while the eternal God will be
the direct cause of all our spiritual transit; for there
will be "no more sea."

But it will be time enough to fly away rapturously,
when we unitedly sing the song of redemption
through Jesus. As for me, I'm here still, riding on
the ocean, and praying for calm weather enough to
allow a few merry "John-Bullites" to go through
the song that they have already attempted to sing a
score of times:

> "I'm on the sea, I'm on the sea,
> The blue, the fresh, the ever free
> It mounts to th . . . .' O, O, dear!"

Every voyager is expected to tell some thrilling
narrative of hair-breadth escape from pirates, from
icebergs, from storm, from wreck, from what not?
Must I submit to this demand? One day our men
harpooned a monstrous fish of some sort, and hauled
him up on deck. Cutting him open, they exhibited
the whole specimen to the ship. This was a great
treat for me, as I had a chance to investigate. With
my large magnifying glass I got down low to examine through my magnifier the millions of parasites
that covered the entire carcass. I was certainly

much interested, acquiring ideas, when all at once
some graceless wag gave my head a violent push
downward, and tumbled me sprawling into the nasty,
slimy fish. However, nobody knew that my name
is "Jonah." Fortunately my fish was fished and
dead.

Something must transpire in the life of every man
to bring him into notice. Soon after this trifling
circumstance, I was obliged to put up with the many
new acquaintances that thrust themselves upon me.
Everybody was blamed for the filthy joke, and of
course nobody knew anything about it. But, beyond this, the people wanted to know something
about me. "Then said they unto him, tell us, we
pray thee, for whose cause this evil is upon us?
What is thine occupation? and whence comest thou?
What is thy country? and of what people art thou?
And he said unto them, I am a Hebrew, and I fear
Jehovah, the God of heaven, which hath made the
sea and the dry land." (Jonah i: 8.) This was my
time to preach Christ, and to prove myself to be a
Christian.

Every name of enemy to the cross of Christ was
represented in this crowd, including six Jews.
Among them I found but two old soldiers of the
cross, who, I afterward learned, belonged to the
Methodist church. They were visiting the United
States to see their children, intending then to return
to their native land and lay their bones in English
soil. When I became fully conscious of the startling
truth that out of two hundred or more persons, but
three even professed to adore the immaculate Jesus,

I resolved, God helping me, I will try to preach the gospel on board this very ship.

One of the common disasters at sea, which teach sinful man that God demands our devotion now fell upon us. After a hard time of four weeks' duration, instead of landing at New York, agreeably to our expectation and prayers, we found ourselves tacking about the banks of Newfoundland. In due time the storm subsided. The ship was very badly shaken; but we were all safe now, and the sea stood calm. How wonderful to see the ship resting peacefully upon the same briny bosom that had heaved with her so tumultuously, even imperiling many precious lives for quite a long time! The great hulk appears to be taking a breathing spell, as she lies straight in her full length, as though glad of a cessation of hostilities with the boisterous elements. All hands fell to work with right good will to right the boat, and soon we were under way again for New York.

"Ebenezer! hitherto the Lord hath helped us." But the thought of all these precious souls rushing upon God with the thick bosses of their buckler, only to be driven back into the fire of His eternal wrath, awakened in my heart a determination to try to save them in the name of the Lord Jesus. Watching for an opportunity when the rough profane captain appeared to be in a good humor, I asked permission to call the passengers and crew together, that I might preach to them the Gospel of Jesus. He replied by swearing sailor-fashion that he did not care what I did, provided I kept on the forward deck of the vessel. At the word, I announced the hour for preaching. The weather being calm at the time, I mounted on a chair which I had placed between the two decks, and reading the thirteenth chapter of Luke's gospel, proceeded for the first time in my life to select a text, namely, the third verse, "Except ye repent, ye shall all likewise perish." I then tried to tell them just what the Lord communicated to me.

It must here be understood that I had no protection. The captain, a demon at the head of a ship load of willing dupes, while I was speaking, every imaginable annoyance was practised for my confusion. As the first class there were four infidels. The second class included six Jews. Among the third class were about eighty Catholics; and they were the most reverential in their conduct. The Jews chased the dogs, set the pigs squealing, and tumbled against my chair—by accident. The infidels derided and debated to nobody's advantage: while the sailors and their inferiors cursed, looking at me and swearing by turns. Still I stuck to it, and preached Christ. God knows that it was a feeble but sincere effort. That I might not be altogether cast down in my virgin endeavor, God gave me one sailor, and a happier convert I have not yet seen. This filled me with such courage that, from such a small beginning, I continued to preach Jesus, and to this day I have not ceased to declare the unsearchable riches of Christ.

This new labor exposed me to new trials. The Jews and infidels united to annoy me. But God was my very present help in trouble. I did not fear.

And after a hard voyage of nearly ten weeks, we anchored at the quarantine, some time toward the last of September, of the cholera season in 1834. Two weeks later, we were permitted to land in New York. Now, I am a pilgrim indeed!

CHAPTER XXVI.

MY SELF-SELECTED HOME.

"Each aspiration of our human earth
Becomes an act thro' keenest pangs of birth;
Each force, to bless, must cease to be a dream,
And conquer life thro' agony supreme."

This day I step upon American soil. Little did I at that time dream that here I was to spend the remainder of my days. It was not the appearance of the city that filled my soul with misgivings. But, "I'm a pilgrim, and I'm a stranger." Nor was it this fact alone: but, a stranger, I am withal very poor. Even yet I have not told the whole truth. I am both poor and proud. Fearful forebodings control my whole soul in remembrance of my brother's prediction, that I would beg my bread from door to door in America. A poor emigrant! where shall I go? what shall I do? aye, what *can* I do? "Beg!" chuckled Satan. Never! "though He slay me, yet will I trust in *Him*." Still I could not help praying for a passage back to my own country. But I had no home there. Yet my heart was there. Nobody in New York surely cared for an outcast, Christian, Jewish boy. True, I had a church letter, but what could I do with it? I had no *home*, and my spirits were sorely dejected. I dare not make myself

254

known. Perhaps the church would have been my shelter from the storm. But I had no experience, and was too proud besides to have any living being know of my condition. No, I will "stand still and see the salvation of the Lord." I will submit to my destiny, whatever be the will of the Lord, whether prosperity or adversity.

In those days there were few Christian hands and hearts wide open to receive the foreigner who lands upon the free soil of the new world; if there had been, I should not have lain nearly three weeks in a miserable house, sick with cholera, without the aid of human hand or sympathy of Christian prayer. So at least it seemed. But my "Friend, who sticketh closer than a brother," never deserted me. Had I died then, my name would have been blotted from earth's record. Nobody knew me, nobody cared for me. They would have said, "a pauper has died." "Rattle his bones," etc.

While I was lying sick in helplessness and filth, at just such an outside place as you may well imagine they would thrust a dying emigrant into, even then I did not realize that I should die. Jesus restored unto me the joy of His salvation, and for His sake I recovered, to speak forth the honor of His glorious name to a perishing world. When, however, I recovered, I had to submit to the loss of one of my trunks, which had been stolen. Thus I lost nearly all my clothes; certainly all my best things. But there was no redress.

My afflictions began to feel heavy, but the remembrance that Jesus endured agony far heavier than I could sustain, and all this to encourage me, certainly made my burden light. Was this the way to take the *yoke* of Christ upon me? Jesus at least sanctified all my distress to me, and gave me grace to rehearse all my sorrows in the ears of my Lord.

My money was now nearly exhausted. I did not know how to make more. I cried to the Lord in my extremity. I knew not where else to go. "In my distress I called upon the Lord and cried to my God; He heard my voice out of His temple, and my cry came before Him, even into His ears." I felt assured that relief would come in a way that I knew not. Early next morning, I shouldered my all, and embarked for Philadelphia.

One entire day of the journey was occupied with thoughts about what would come next, five dollars of my little stock of money being paid for my fare, leaving only fifty-eight cents to begin life with. But I must grapple with the prospect, trusting in the Lord. It was quite late in the night when we arrived at the city of brotherly love. Once more I am on strange ground, now after dark with fifty-eight cents total in my pocket. My trunk was seized by a man. "Follow me," and he led on, "I'll take you to a stopping place." What else could I do? After a short walk he left me for the night, charging me thirty-seven cents for his labor. With the remaining twenty-one cents in my pocket, I fell down in agony before my God, and then attempted to obtain rest, but I could not sleep. I soon discovered that the house was of a dubious character. My soul was wrought up to the very highest pitch. Everything with me was now at stake, my trunk, my life, and above all, my Christian name. I fell on my knees and wept out my troubles before my God. Nor did I pray in vain. While I was yet wrestling the Lord heard me; and blessed be His name, He flew to my deliverance that very night. The dread of begging was entirely dissipated. I felt calm, assured that the Lord had not forsaken me.

Very early in the morning, I was disposed to walk out; I knew not why nor where. Paying the woman twelve cents for my bed, I politely asked her to take care of my trunk, and noting well the location of the house, with nine (9) cents, it being all the money I had in the world, I started out with light heart and easy step. I did not know where to go, but the Lord knew where to direct me, and He directed me to a sure provision.

The city was not yet astir, but see how wonderfully the Lord controls man in His own behalf. Walking on Market Street, I noticed the sign over a store, advertising the business to be, manufacturing "ladies' furs and men's caps." Now, although my father was a furrier, yet I did not understand the business, having never made a cap in my life. Still something said to me, "You will succeed there; don't go away; wait awhile; courage!" I waited a long time, at least it seemed so, and feeling was my watch. After a while, however, a man came out to open the shutters. I walked up to him and inquired whether a man was wanted here as journeyman. "I guess so," audibly thought he, "the boss discharged a jour on last Saturday night for getting

17

drunk; you had better stay and see the boss, he'll be along after awhile." My heart leaped, as certain of success. I waited with little patience until half past nine, when lo, in came the boss. The man gave me the wink, and in a moment I was at his side. I made my business known. "How do you know I want a hand? who told you?" I related to him how that I was a stranger. The short of it is this; I was employed at once, on trial until Saturday night, at the rate of eight dollars a week, and if I gave satisfaction, then permanently. Saturday night duly came. I had given entire satisfaction, and was employed at good wages. God helped me and I did well. Hallelujah to my Almighty Friend, who saved me from the pangs of beggary, and even want. Long as I live, I remember this incident, I speak about it, I cannot forget it: my heart feels grateful this day for it, and I feel that I shall bless His holy name forever, who spared me from begging my bread. And now that I am old and poor for Christ's sake, I know that the Lord will not let me beg my bread; yet I cannot repeat too frequently, "Though He slay me yet will I trust in Him."

After one week I began to feel quite settled and independent. With a calm mind and happy heart, I felt that I might with propriety now offer myself to the First Baptist Church for membership. It was then under the pastorate of Rev. William Brantly, D. D., of blessed memory. Some time during the following year, namely 1835, the Church furnished me with a letter certifying their approbation of my character and design to prepare myself by "appropriate studies" to enter at a future day upon the solemn work of the Christian ministry. Four years later, on the 18th of December, 1839, in the Baptist Church at Mount Pleasant, Westmoreland County, Pa., I was fully ordained to the sacred office. The Council for the occasion were, Rev. S. Siegfried, Moderator, Rev. James Estep, Rev. Milton Sutton, and Rev. John Thomas. On behalf of the Church, part was taken by Deacon A. Shallenbarger and Jonathan Newmyer.

CHAPTER XXVII

WAY NOTES.

I have at the date of this publication arrived at the time of life which passes sentence on childhood and youth, that they "are vanity." Not, however, in dotage, I am rather notional. A few days ago, I laid down my pen, having "finished" this little book: drawing a long breath, I said, good bye, severe penance of writing so much about little self; I will put my "Poetical Prophet" in order, and so close. But am not I notional; or do I simply feel the force of the truth, that people are never satisfied? The trite, true adage, "The more we have, the more we want," has been attested whenever I have told my Christian experience to a congregation. Great as may be the objection to long sermons, I have never seen impatience during any length of time occupied by my narration; but on the contrary, am constantly beset by questions. Now I assure you, modest reader, that I would rather stand fire than answer all these; but as I never could have my choice in the matter, I have always braced myself for the wretched ordeal, put on as pleasant a face as I could very well muster, and await the issue. Ah me! I would not have long to wait: on it comes. The ladies are smiling so sweetly, sometimes ogling, always blushing; and their twittering, accompanied by a few inuendoes, half expressed and temptingly withdrawn, all taper off into the culminating point. "Elder Davis," ventures one of the senior ladies, generally the mother, "Elder Davis, the girls here want to know whether finally you married that M.?" Then follows a general good-natured laugh, as they listen to my equally good-natured. reply. Well no, I didn't marry her at all; you see that "man proposes but God disposes," but I even didn't propose after I lost all my property: so I came to this country, and in my twenty-seventh year I married a lady in Pennsylvania.

Now, my notion is to save myself further tribulation of such loquacious character, and yet gratify the reader's curiosity in a manner as philosophical as Ben Franklin's proposition to his father "to ask one big blessing over the whole beef at once, and thus save the trouble of asking so many little blessings over small pieces.

I had been in Philadelphia about three years, making a good living and serving the Lord as well as I could, by preaching Christ without human endorsement, and traveling on quite easily, independently of my relations. Hitherto I had not written to my father, as I resolved to bring him, if possible, to reflection by my silence. About this time, however, there was an advertisement for me in one of the public papers. I was thus informed if I would call on Mr. I. I., at No.—— —— street, Philadelphia, I should hear something to my advantage. I obeyed the summons, and found a Jewish gentleman whom I knew in boyhood. He said that this was the evidence of my father's attachment for me, and then immediately attempted to put me through an examination, by asking more questions than I felt willing to answer. I did not like his manner, and, therefore, he could not catch me asleep. He requested me to call again, but did not say what he wanted me for. As I was then quite independent, I thought it inadvisable to trouble myself further, and so I let it pass.

A few months after this, I received a letter from my brother in London, containing no point of public interest whatever, excepting the demand that my letters *must* be directed to *him*, and that I must be silent about religion. His very immodest words are almost sufficient to deter me from giving them to a Christian public. I risk the exposure as disclosing modern Judaism. His letter, dated London, June 16th, 1835, is at present before me to substantiate all I write. He comments thus, " You ask me, have I been anxious to hear from you? Yes! and you have, as on every other occasion, acted in so absurd a manner that all my energies can but pronounce your letter a posse of d—d stuff emanating from an unsound mind," etc. The receipt of such a letter, in reply to mine which affectionately preached Christ, so disgusted and discouraged me that I did not write to him again for several years.

About ten years after this, I received a letter from my father in reply to one from me. He apologizes for not being able to write more than his name, on account of infirmities. His old clerk, the miserable infidel, acted as his amanuensis. In this letter he refers me to the time, now about eight years ago, when Mr. I. I. was in America.

He says that he felt anxious about me, and that the long silence has been my own fault. This I acknowledge, and the reader will understand my motive after reading an extract from his letter. "Not the least of my anxieties has been caused by your secession from the Holy Religion of your fathers, which you must naturally suppose has been a source of grief to me and all our family. Such being the case, I therefore particularly request that you will in future abstain from making any comments on religion. You have thought proper to forsake the one in which you were born, and in which all your ancestors have lived and died, and as you cannot persuade me either to approve of the step or to imitate the example, it will be much better not to reintroduce the subject in your future correspondence, particularly as a recurrence to it will be most painful to my feelings, as it also is to every other member of the family. No arguments on your part will induce any of us to forego a faith which has through evil report and good report, stood the test of ages, and which has the Scripture for its foundation; therefore let all future correspondence be carried on without recurring to a subject upon which we can never agree, and which is only annoying to all our feelings. Although I sincerely deplore your apostacy from the religion of your forefathers, my natural feelings as a parent will always cause me to experience the liveliest pleasure in hearing of your welfare, and to hope

that as now the correspondence has commenced, you
will not fail to write occasionally."—In this letter
my father seems to talk quite conciliatorily. He
speaks very kindly of my wife and children. I felt
that I had gained my point in establishing my independence for Christ's sake: I had lived without
father's help, and had not once asked for bed or
bread. I could therefore afford to continue a correspondence. In later letters, however, I was again admonished to be quiet about religion. Ultimately,
father begs leave to " agree to disagree."

Finding myself effectually silenced in argument, I
had no future resort but to be very still-tongued
about religion. Three years later, in 1848, I am in
receipt of a letter from my father, in which he ac-
knowledges the receipt of my family group in da-
guerreotype, and promises a return compliment. In
that letter I am made the happy recipient of some
very choice blessings for myself and family. Such
Christless blessings, however, could not penetrate
my " turned-coat:" still they did me no harm. Letters continued to cross the ocean, but no Christ
was in them all: neither was I permitted even to re-
vert to religion at all. At one time, my father would
inform me that it is of no consequence what a man's
religion consists of; at another time, Judaism alone
was scriptural: but I never received from home *a
single scripture quotation.* At the same time, my
maddened brother pronounced my letters to be " stuff
emanating out of an unsound mind." Every one of
my letters that contained the most distant reference
to the Christian religion, was treated with the same

insulting disrespect by every member of the several families. Thus my letters were *driven to Christless-ness!* Apart from religion, my correspondence with my relations was pleasant, so much so, that about this time I received large daguerreotypes of my elder sister and father, and subsequently my father sent me his portrait, taken in oil colors.

For some time past my father's health had been evidently failing, and on March 10th, 1851, a letter was written by my brother, containing the information that my father was dying. Soon after, I received another letter, informing me that, "Your dear father ceased to exist on the morning of Wednesday, March the 26th, at nine o'clock:" and on the 30th of April, I received another letter from my brother, who was one of the executors of the will, favoring me with a quotation therefrom. It ran thus: "I will and bequeath to my son Jonas A. Davis the sum of one hundred pounds—and I limit that bequest to the said sum of one hundred pounds, only because he displeased me during my life." It further states that "the bequest of the one hundred pounds shall be demanded in person or by writing duly authenticated by affidavit, within the *space of three years* from the day of his death: otherwise he will lose all claim on the estate." During next month another letter was sent West, and then one more, dated June 23d, again informing me of my legacy and as before, quoting from the will, "he having disobliged me during my life."

Thus it appears that although I "displeased" my dear father, and "disobliged" him by my acceptance of the Messiah as my Saviour, he did leave me more than "a shilling." I had no reason to complain: there awaited my acceptance the wonderful sum of $500.

Hitherto every letter I received was affectionately addressed to me, but a letter written on September 8th, 1851, by my brother, declared that a persecuting spirit still existed. When I left home in 1834, my father's second family was increasing rapidly. A dear little half brother of four years of age did not understand my troubles. For some years past, he had been in New York. My father, who informed me of the fact, requested that I should not try to convert him to the Christian religion. I wrote to him in New York, but received no reply. But now, my father being dead, I ventured to write to my half brother, and proposed investigating the subject of religion. I soon received a reply in this shape: the envelope contained my letter returned, and inside the envelope were written the words, by somebody unknown to me, "No further communication required." I felt sorry for my baby brother. Toward the first of October, I received another letter from my brother, in London, which explained the whole farce. I give an extract. "My dear brother ——, of New York, has informed me that he had received a letter from you, and also forwarded extracts from the same. They are vile and hypocritical, and I commend him for the way he served your letter." This letter addresses me with simply "Sir." I did not reply to the insult, but a very serious matter of talk in my family was my paying a visit to my relations in England. I was very slow about deciding the question. My wife, however, assisted me in this affair by deciding affirmatively, pleading that I ought to see my relations once more. Still I was slow about moving, and did not get started until the 21st of June, 1852.

Although at this time my family were well provided for until I should, in the providence of God, return to them, still when the hour came to say, "good bye," I repented my bargain. Many a time counsel had been asked of God. No plain, approving indications were given to me. There were misgivings in my heart. I felt oppressed at the idea of leaving my wife and two small children, the firstborn a daughter then in her thirteenth year, the second a son in his eleventh year. But it is decided I must go, to be back again so soon as possible. My heart palpitates; time is up. Once more on our knees: "Lord, protect them." One more choking, good bye kiss—and I'm off. Visions of that cherub daughter, standing petrified on the floor with eyes riveted on her father as he leaves the house, haunted me, followed me, never left me, and are before me now.

My passage is paid, I am actually aboard, I feel like a weaned child. Sad at heart, I moan; I write a hasty note to send home. I feel crushed, I am miserable; I *must* return home again. "Captain," sighed some one, "I give up this voyage; I'm going home again. Please put me and my goods ashore. I don't want my passage money refunded, only let me go off the ship." Vain pleading! The tender hearts of the "jolly tars" did actually sympathize with me. They said that I "should feel better in an hour or two after we had left the shore." I yielded to their persuasion, and entered the cabin with the captain.

We are off now, but I am still miserable. Sea-sickness comes to my relief, but I am none the better for this, save that for the time I cannot think of either wife or child. Let me die!—But I must not, and in due time the staunch sailor arrived in the London docks.

Ashore again in my native land, I would have given worlds to fly back again over the ocean to America. But it is too late to retreat now. I must settle down, attend to business, and preach Messiah. The first thing was a letter for home. The next was to visit at a prayer meeting in the Spencer Place Church. I am recognized after an absence of eighteen years, have seen my old pastor, Rev. Mr. Peacock, and some of the older members. Bearing testimony for Jesus, I already feel at home.

My next business was to go see my brother. He is found living in elegant style among the notables, at the West end of the city. I am now standing silent before him. I knew him, but he paused a minute to recognize me. "Jonas," and we were in each other's arms. We soon began to talk over matters in amicable spirit, he treating me well, after a fashion. The hospitalities of his house were not tendered me, but he said he would be glad to see me every time I called. I was found to be quite ready to defend my religion, but he requested me to say nothing about it. So I yielded to very superior argument and was shut off. Nevertheless, he was kind to me, and assisted me in reaching other members of the family. I found that the estate of my father was not yet balanced; it would require some further time. I was, however, received as a minister of Jesus by the Christian community, and thus sustained.

Finding that my business in London was likely to be a long job, I immediately wrote to my wife to break up house-keeping and come to me. She received my letter in due time, and out of time a letter came for me. I tremble. But, why? My heart misgives me. I open it. O God! death has invaded *my* home. On the twenty-fifth of October, 1852, my dear little daughter, my cherub, first-born died! On the fourteenth of the next month, my afflicted wife started with the only child, and he just taken sick with the same fever that killed his sister. But for the merciful providence of God, she had not in safety crossed Lake Erie. The boat expected at Cleveland, to make a connection for Dunkirk, was late arriving. In consequence of the unfinished condition of the Lake Shore road, my wife was obliged to travel one entire day by stage. The boat at last arrived, took in her freight, started to cross the lake, but never arrived at her destination.—Arriving in New York, she took passage in the steamship City of Glasgow, of ill-fated memory. When about mid-ocean, Captain Wyley was aroused one night by the cry of " fire." He was a Christian, and with the utmost calmness moved about noiselessly, while with annihilators he extinguished the fire, the passengers meanwhile sleeping. After a voyage of seventeen days, arrival was safely effected in London. This ship returned safely, but on her re-visit to the Old World, with four hundred passengers on board of her, she was lost. And " no man knoweth" her " sepulchre to this day." O man, " prepare to meet thy God."

Now we are all together once more. All together? No, no! Our commingled groans and tears but too sadly declared that our first-born was dead. She sickened on Thursday, and her spirit rose to the Lord with the rising sun of Monday. "He giveth; He taketh: He doeth all things well." Many days and many nights listened to the discussion of our theme —our dead daughter!!! After I left home, she appeared to take the supervision of her father's things. They might not be removed from the corner or place where " father left them." Hers was the language of mature faith, " God can take care of father on the sea as well as on the land." And many a childish petition was lifted up from her beautiful heart, by angel hands laid carefully on the wings of the Spirit of God, and thus wafted into the presence-chamber of the Eternal, lisping, breathing, weeping, " O Heavenly Father, take care of my father." When she knew that scarlet fever would kill her, she said in hope as well as resignation, " I shall see my Father in heaven before I see my earthly father." And when she felt the grasp of death, she gasped, " Jesus has pardoned all my sins—*all* my sins."

" There is no death; what seems so is transition:
    This life of mortal breath
Is like a suburb, to the life Elysian,
    Whose portal we call death.

" She is not dead, the child of our affections,
    But gone into that school
Where she no longer needs our poor corrections,
    For Christ Himself doth rule."

We remained in England about eight months after my wife arrived, our hearts all the time yearning, longing, and praying for the time when we should return to the United States. Law work in England moves slowly, so that I had to bide my time. I could have borne even this disappointment, had not a far greater trouble tormented me. My relations would not see my wife, because she was not a Jewess. "This was the most unkindest cut of all." I felt sad at first, as I reviewed the ground. I had told all about my wife's troubles. I said, Her only daughter died after three days' illness: then she herself was seized by the same fever most malignantly, so that she could not move on the day of her daughter's funeral: the lone coffin was carried on the arms of friends: mother was not there; father was more than 3500 miles distant; but on the arms of friendship fraternal the little son, the only child, was carried, that he might see how ruthlessly the grave can separate him from his only, his precious sister for all time: that on the very day when she started to travel, the little boy was taken sick, and continued ill during the voyage: that she endured all this alone, and finally, by the mercy of Almighty, reached me in safety.

I would have forgiven them ten times, aye until seventy times seven, for all the wrongs they had heaped upon me, if only they had taken my afflicted wife into their affections. Their assistance I did not need in any form. Christians supplied my need, while I preached Christ. I only wanted their sympathy. Would they treat my wife with common humanity? No! They could not, they would not, they did not. Alas! *she was not a Jewess.* I argued with them, "You are supported by the Gentiles; you keep company with them when you make money off them—what harm then can my Christian wife do you?" No matter, they did not see her once, because *she was a Christian.* This treatment amounted to nothing less than insult to my wife; but toward me personally it wore the phase of disgustingly ignorant persecution. I concluded, therefore, that my brother, who took the trouble to send me a letter across the ocean, informing me that I am a hypocrite—now that in my extreme affliction he acted so hypocritically toward me, did but little credit to the religion he professed, and was unworthy of my friendship. I called on him to say, good bye, and have not corresponded with him since our return to the United States, nearly seventeen years ago.

My younger sister lived in Dublin, at the head of a noble family. Presently I received a letter from her, stating that her house was full of company, so that she could not then entertain me; "but," said she, "come after the fair." Doubtless my sister meant all she said: I, however, felt too much op-

pressed by such ill-timed treatment to move out of
my way. I did not visit her, but on the fifth of
June, 1853, we took passage in the Tuscarora, and
after a rough voyage of five weeks, we landed in
Philadelphia.

18

CHAPTER XXVIII.

THOMAS, AND I.

At this point, I will fulfil my promise, and write a few lines about "the boy Thomas." Several years before my mention of him, he entered father's establishment as shop, or warehouse boy. (I dare not speak about his aspirations, because these are almost wholly unknown to a poor boy in England.) Here he was doomed to serve an apprenticeship and learn nothing. He was a loquacious, under-sized, "west country" youth, heavy built, and rather bow-legged. But, uncomely as he was, he surpassed Shakspeare's "toad" which had a "precious jewel in its head." Thomas had one in his heart: he was honest. As time passed on, Thomas evidently learned the Christian law of progress, "Giving all diligence, add to your faith virtue, and to virtue knowledge, and to knowledge temperance, and to temperance patience, and to patience Godliness, and to Godliness brotherly kindness, and to brotherly kindness charity." He was always spoken of as a "good boy," and no uneasiness was ever experienced about the affairs of the house if Thomas was about. My father well knew that he received far more than an equivalent for the miserable pittance he paid him. Nobody ever

274

dreamed that it was the power of the Christian religion which made Thomas so valuable a servant.

Surrounded by Jews, he could not so well speak of the Christian religion. This would not be for a moment tolerated in my father's establishment. But his general behavior was so exemplary, that it required but few words from Thomas to operate as a corrective to the immoral utterances of his fellow employees of either sex. Poor fellow! how those wicked Gentiles used to torment him. It was during one of my relaxations from school duties, that I employed my leisure time (and there was much of it) in uniting with his tormentors. One day I had drank my ale, according to custom, but having taken a little too much—Tom, taunted I, Tom, I say, Tom; Tom—you're a fool. He looked sternly at me and replied, " Master Davis, 'you must be born again.' " Ha, ha, ha; born again! I tell you you're a fool, and if you talk any more nonsense to me, I'll put your head into that dog-trough. Now be it known, that said Thomas was much stouter than myself, and could have given me a sound drubbing, although we were about the same age: but the weapons of his warfare were not carnal; in fact I did not know the secret of his power—he prayed for me. Heedless of consequences, he forthwith repeated the declaration, " 'You must be born again.' " I must, eh? you fool; and making a sudden spring, I seized him by the throat and threw him, his head striking against the dog-trough, and making a mess generally. My ale worked well! We were on our feet the same instant. I thought he looked angry. I expected a flogging, for I deserved it, and he could have accomplished it. Instead, he only wiped his face, pale with emotion, saying, " Master Davis, I pray for you; I'll tell my Heavenly Father of you." Here I grew devilish. You Christian dog—you—you—. But he is off. I howled after him, Tom! Tom! you're a fool.

This, with much more like it, was brought to my mind after the scene narrated in my history. But now I am in London: I have my wife by my side: we are walking, having resorted to this expedient to relieve our minds. I point to the house of my birth, the house of my first prayers, and the spot of ground whereon I stood, to receive my father's curse, counteracted, however, by angel's songs and God's blessings. We go to visit Thomas, whom I found in the city. Father's old place of business had passed into other hands, still I found many there who respected his memory. Some time before I engaged to preach a few months for a country church, I held service every Lord's day in London, and Thomas was a constant hearer. . . . . .

It is the history of conversion that forms the focus of a life. This you have, with antecedents and consequences. The routine of an humble pastorate or two, could but show a plain and matter of fact outworking of those new-found principles already boldly sketched.

In hastening these pages to a close, I do not doubt that I have exhausted my reader's patience, while leading him through the various meanderings of my Christian experience. Faithfully have I endeavored to unfold the providences of my God in bringing me, a poor lost rebel, to the glorious light of the Gospel of Jesus. Whether the reader believes these details or not, "one thing I know, that whereas I was blind, now I see." And during the interval of thirty-four years, I have not once felt gloomy on account of my religion. I do not know what regret means. Thus far the Lord hath brought me, and I will trust Him for the future.

What now "think *ye* of Christ?" Soon, alas, too soon, my unregenerated reader will be summoned to His eternal bar. O Israel, why did you crucify your King? You must see Him, to know Him. You will look upon Him whom you have pierced, (for "they (Israel) pierced my (Messiah's) hands and feet:") and wail for anguish of heart, for your destruction will then have come! O, fly to your own Shiloh. In Him alone you may find eternal life.

And dear Gentile reader, why dost thou reject the blessed Jesus? Has not He suffered and died for you also? What more can be done? "How *shall* we escape if we neglect *so great salvation?*" Stop, traveler, think, oh think of the day, the dark and fiery day, the great day of revelation that will burn as an oven. It will destroy your expectation as stubble!

Jesus, blessed Saviour, thou hast saved me; now hear me, precious Redeemer, stretch forth Thy hand and save each unchristian reader.

But child of grace, let us rejoice together, for He hath both wounded and healed us. Soon, very soon we shall behold Him in glory. Even now we are freed from the horrible pit, and never will He suffer us to fall into it again. Then with our goings established, and our feet upon the rock, let us travel on together, singing the new song, and " looking unto Jesus, the one Messiah."

THE POETICAL PROPHET.

Gen. 49 : 10.	The Sceptre shall be Judah's boon	John 11 : 48.
	Till the Messiah rise,	John 11 : 52.
Ps. 68 : 18.	With men the Lord will then commune;	Ac. 1 : 9.
Isa. 11 : 1.	From David forth He hies.	Mat. 1 : 17.
Isa. 7 : 14.	Conceived by spotless virgin maid,	Lk. 1 : 27.
Mic. 5 : 2.	In Bethlehem brought forth,	Lk. 2 : 15.
Ps. 72 : 10.	By kings is homage to Him paid	Mat. 2 : 8.
Isa. 60 : 6.	And gathered nations' worth.	Mat. 2 : 11.
Jer. 31 : 15.	For Him graves cradle infant bloom,	Mat. 2 : 16.
Hos. 11 : 1.	While Egyptward He hastes;	Mat. 2 : 14.
Mal. 3 : 1.	A messenger for Him makes room	Lk. 3 : 4.
Isa. 40 : 3.	And gladdening, threads drear wastes.	Mk. 1 : 2.
Isa. 53 : 7.	The perfect Lamb of God is He,	John 1 : 36.
Isa. 35 : 5.	By whom are wonders wrought—	Lk. 7 : 14.
Isa. 29 : 18.	The deaf shall hear, the blind shall see:	Mat. 11 : 5.
Isa. 12 : 2.	God comes to save unsought.	Lk. 2 : 30.
Jer. 16 : 16	Poor fishermen to serve Him vie;	Mat. 10 : 1.
Isa. 6 : 9.	In parables He'll teach;	Mat. 13 : 34.
Ps. 68 : 27.	Capernaum and Naphtali	Mat. 4 : 13.
Isa. 9 : 1.	With Zebul'n hear Him preach.	Mat. 4 : 15.
Joel 2 : 26.	Might from His hand bread multiplies;	Mat. 15 : 33.
Zech. 9 : 9.	His triumph's humbly borne:	Mk. 11 : 7.
Ps. 2 : 2.	Against Him kings and rulers rise	Mk. 15 : 1.
Isa. 53 : 5.	Down pouring sin and scorn.	Mat. 27 : 50.
Isa. 53 : 10.	For us will He be bruised and die;	Mat. 27 : 26.
Zech. 13 : 7.	Dispersed His bleating flock:	Mat. 26 : 56.
Dan. 9 : 24.	Both time and place foretold we spy,	Mat. 1 : 17.
Ps. 109 : 6.	And Judah's treacherous shock.	Mk. 14 : 43.

Zech. 11 : 12.	For thirty silver pieces sold,	Mat. 26 : 15.
Ps. 27 : 12.	False witnesses accuse;	Mat. 26 : 59.
Isa. 53 : 5.	They buffet Him, they taunt, blindfold,	Lk. 22 : 64.
Isa. 50 : 6.	And spitting, much abuse.	Mat. 27 : 30.
Ps. 27 : 2.	The wicked now the just surround:	Mat. 27 : 27.
Isa. 53 : 5.	Stripes wound His flesh and tear:	Mat. 27 : 26.
Lam. 3 : 14.	Scorn and derision past all bound,	Mat. 27 : 41.
	With bitterness He'll bear.	Mat. 27 : 44.
Isa. 53 : 12.	His name with trespassers enroll;	Mk. 15 : 28.
Ex. 32 : 32.	For such He'll intercede:	Lk. 23 : 34.
Numb. 21 : 8.	As brazen serpent on the pole	John 3 : 14.
	They set Him up with speed.	Mat. 27 : 35.
Ps. 22 : 16.	His hands and feet pierced by the nail,	John 19 : 18.
Numb. 9 : 12.	A bone they shall not break:	John 19 : 33.
Ps. 22 : 7.	With wagging heads they at Him rail,	Mat. 27 : 39.
Ps. 22 : 18.	His clothes by lot they take.	John 19 : 23.
Isa. 53 : 8.	They put to death the Prince of life,	Lk. 23 : 33.
Ps. 16 : 10.	But death He'll vanquish quite,	John 20 : 19.
Isa. 25 : 8	In triumph rising o'er earth's strife,	John 20 : 14.
Isa. 9 : 7.	Possessed of untold might.	Mat. 28 : 18.

APPENDIX.

LICENSE TO PREACH.

The Regular Baptist Church of Christ, at Mount Pleasant, Westmoreland County, Pennsylvania,

To All Whom it May Concern:

Whereas, Our esteemed brother, Jonas Abraham ·Davis, formerly a member of the First Baptist Church of the City of Philadelphia, was by the said Church, in December, A. D. 1835, furnished with a letter certifying their approbation of his character and design to prepare himself by appropriate studies "to enter at a future day upon the solemn work of the Christian Ministry;" and,

Whereas, The said Brother Davis has since united with us, and been encouraged to exercise his gifts in preaching the Gospel, and has given comfortable evidence of the possession of piety, character, and talents fitting him, in a good degree, to enter more fully into the work of a Gospel Minister:

We Hereby Certify that the aforesaid brother, Jonas Abraham Davis, has received from us a full license to go forth as a Minister of the Gospel, of the Regular Baptist Denomination, to preach the word of eternal life, wherever God, in His providence, may call him; and we commend him to the fellowship of the brethren, and to the confidence and esteem of all among whom he may labor or travel in the Master's service. Our prayer is that he may become an able Minister of the New Testament, and be blessed as an instrument in the building up of believers in their most holy faith, and in turning many to righteousness.

Voted, at our stated meeting for business, May 11th, A. D., 1839.

SIMEON SIEGFRIED, Pastor.

Attest:

A. SHALLENBERGER, } Deacons.
JONA. NEWMYER, }

CERTIFICATE OF ORDINATION.

THIS IS TO CERTIFY, that at the request of, and in connection with, the Regular Baptist Church of Jesus Christ, at Mount Pleasant, Westmoreland County, Pennsylvania, on the eighteenth day of December, A. D., eighteen hundred and thirty-nine, the bearer hereof, Jonas Abraham Davis, was by us regularly ordained and set apart to the office of a Gospel Minister, of the Regular Baptist Denomination; and we do hereby recommend him as a regular, sound, and faithful Minister of the Gospel, to the attention, fellowship, and Christian love of all the Churches of our denomination in particular; to the notice and respect of all Ministers and other Christians of other denominations; and to the respectful acceptance of mankind in general; hoping that he will be kindly received, and blessed by God in his labors, wherever, in Divine Providence, his lot may be cast.

Given under our hands, the date aforesaid.

S. SIEGFRIED, *Moderator.*

JAMES ESTEP,
MILTON SUTTON, } *Council.*
JOHN THOMAS,

On behalf of the Church,

A. SHALLENBERGER, } *Deacons.*
JONA. NEWMYER,

www.ingramcontent.com/pod-product-compliance
Lightning Source LLC
Chambersburg PA
CBHW030628030726
47497CB00006B/1692